POSH

★

PASTA

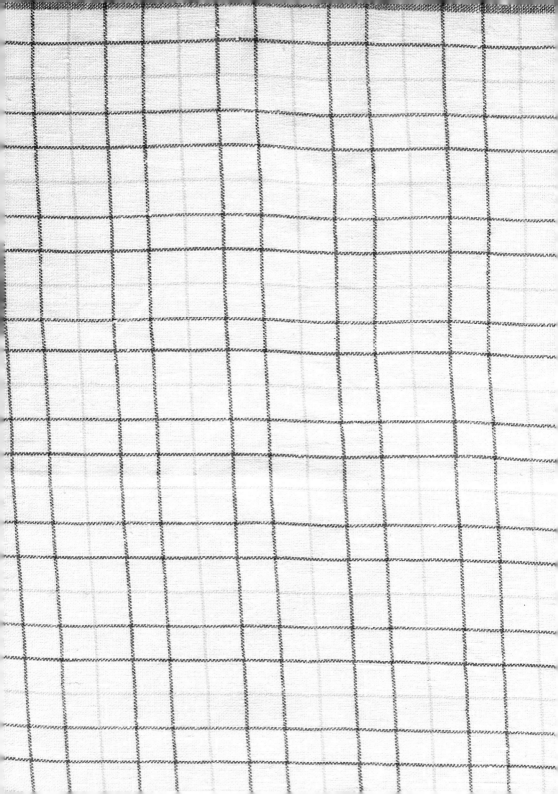

POSH
PASTA

Over 70 recipes, from perfect
pappardelle to tempting tortellini

Pip Spence

Photography by Faith Mason

Hardie Grant

QUADRILLE

Publishing Director: Sarah Lavelle
Series Designer: Gemma Hayden
Designer: Alicia House
Food Stylist and Recipe Writer: Pip Spence
Photographer: Faith Mason
Props Stylist: Rachel Vere
Production Controller: Katie Jarvis
Head of Production: Stephen Lang

Published in 2020 by Quadrille,
an imprint of Hardie Grant Publishing

Quadrille
52–54 Southwark Street
London SE1 1UN
quadrille.com

Cataloguing in Publication Data: a catalogue
record for this book is available from the
British Library.

ISBN: 978 1 78713 546 8

Printed in China

CONTENTS

— ✦ —

INTRODUCTION

Pasta in its many forms is one of the most satisfying things to eat in my opinion. Whatever shape or size, sauce or filling, it brings a warmth and a joy from the first forkful. I love pasta! I'm not Italian (and some of the recipes in this book most definitely aren't!), but I appreciate the versatility and function of pasta to be as humble or as posh as you want to make it.

Every base is covered in this book... midweek meals that are heavy on the greens, hearty soups, comforting bakes and classic combinations with a twist. Hopefully something for everyone!

As I wrote these recipes, I called on hints and tips that I've been lucky enough to gather from brilliant pasta chefs (some of them genuinely Italian) over the years.

Buy quality ingredients – I don't mean the most expensive ingredients, but if you're making a pasta dish with only 6 ingredients, say, they may as well be the best you can find.

Canned whole plum tomatoes are preferable to chopped, as they generally contain riper, sweeter tomatoes and the can contains less water. Buy a piece of Parmesan instead of pre-grated – it'll last for ages wrapped in the fridge and the rind can be popped into sauces and soups for extra flavour.

Pasta shapes – Different shapes of pasta work better with different sauces. Long noodles like linguine and spaghetti work so well coated in smooth or creamy sauces. Flatter, wider strands like pappardelle catch chunkier sauces such as ragù. Tube-shaped pastas, like rigatoni and penne, also work well in creamier sauces. Tiny grain-shaped pastas suit soups and salads. But it's all down to personal preference!

Gluten-free and egg-free pasta – there are so many types of gluten-free pasta on the market these days made with lots of interesting alternatives to pasta flour. All of the recipes in this book can swap out regular pasta for your favourite gluten-free. Egg-free pasta is widely available and you can make your own at home by swapping out the egg for a mixture of water and olive oil.

Fresh pasta – there's an in-depth recipe for making your own fresh pasta on page 8. It's quite simple once you get going. Always dust the pasta in fine semolina as you go to stop it from sticking and drying out. Fresh pasta cooks in 2–4 minutes. You can serve it simply with just a little melted butter and a sprinkling of cracked black pepper.

If you're making noodles, you can dry them out to cook later. You can hang them on a clean clothes airer in a cool, dry room until dry (it usually takes 6 hours–overnight). Some pasta can also be dried in nests; place the nests on a cooling rack and make sure they are ventilated from all sides until totally dry. Store dried pasta in a clean airtight container for up to 3 months.

Salt the cooking water – when you come to cook any pasta, make sure you salt the water well. You don't add salt to pasta dough, so if you don't salt the water, it won't taste of very much at all. You don't need to add cooking oil to the water and make sure you use a large pan to boil the pasta. It needs room to move and a good stir while cooking.

Use pasta water to loosen – If you're cooking any hot pasta dish, please, please save a mugful of the starchy water just before you drain. When you're combining your sauce and pasta, a good splash of pasta water brings everything together, keeps the sauce silky and the pasta evenly coated.

Don't let the pasta dry out in the colander – don't cook your pasta too early in the proceedings, as it'll sit there drying out in the colander and just won't be as good as you had hoped. The pasta is often the last thing to cook in the recipe, so just make sure your big pan of salted water is boiling and ready to go!

How to present pasta noodles – a simple and elegant way of presenting pasta like a pro is by using a pair of tongs and a ladle. Use the tongs to pick up a good nest-worth of noodles. Keeping the tongs of noodles in one hand, twist the noodles into the ladle and keep twisting until you have a neat nest. Carefully transfer over to a serving dish, remove the ladle slowly while using the tongs to place the noodles in the dish and you'll have a lovely nest to coat in sauce and add your favourite topping.

What to do with scraps – if you're making pasta and you have a few scraps leftover, you can turn them into a tasty snack like the one on page 118. You can go savoury or sweet with a little drizzle of melted chocolate and a dusting of icing (confectioners') sugar.

BASIC

★

PASTA DOUGH

The general rule of thumb for making pasta is 100g
(3½oz/¾ cup) tipo 00 flour (it's super fine) and 1 egg per
portion, but this depends on what you're using the pasta
for. Filled pastas require less dough per portion than
tagliatelle, for example. When kneading the dough it will
sometimes feel a little dry, so add a little splash of water or
olive oil. It's important to work and rest the dough well in
the fridge; it needs time to develop the gluten.

🍴 SERVES 4–6 (stuffed)
or 8–10 (unstuffed)

🕐 TAKES 15–20 minutes,
plus resting and rolling

400g (14oz/3 cups) tipo 00
   pasta flour
4 large eggs
fine semolina, for dusting
olive oil, if needed

Place the flour in a large bowl and make a well in
the centre. Crack in the eggs and, using a dinner
knife, beat the eggs and gradually bring the flour
into them. Keep mixing and forming lumps of
dough, then use your hands to bring the mixture
together into a ball.

Dust a clean work surface with a little semolina.
Tip the dough on to the work surface and use
your hands and knuckles to knead it until firm
and springy; this may take 5–10 minutes. If it's
still a little dry, add a drop of olive oil or water.

Wrap in cling film (plastic wrap) and place in the
fridge for at least an hour to rest before it's ready
to roll.

method continued overleaf...

★ ★ ★ ★ ★ ★ ★ ★ ★ ★ ★ ★ ★ ★ ★

★ ★

BASIC PASTA DOUGH
continued...

To roll out fresh pasta, ready for stuffing or shaping:

Set up your pasta machine with the rollers on the widest setting. Take the pasta dough from the fridge and cut off a quarter. Roll this through the machine, fold it into thirds and roll again. Do this a few times, then gradually work the pasta sheet through the machine down to the last 2 settings. If making stuffed pasta, it needs to be as thin as your pasta machine will allow. Sheets of dough for shaped pasta can be slightly thicker. If it's not coming together well or you're not happy with the shape of the sheet, don't worry! Just fold the sheet up into thirds so that it'll fit widthways through the machine, set the machine to the thickest setting and start again. Pasta needs to be worked well to develop gluten and improve elasticity (a bit like bread dough).

EASY COLOUR AND FLAVOUR VARIANTS...
Try adding these simple colour and flavour variations to your fresh pasta:

Beetroot (beet)
Add 1 tsp beetroot (beet) powder per 200g (7oz/1½ cups) pasta flour.

Herb
Stir in 2 tbsp chopped parsley, basil or dill per 1 egg just before mixing.

Black pepper
Add 2 tsp freshly ground black pepper per 200g (7oz/1½ cups) pasta flour.

GLUTEN-FREE

★

PASTA DOUGH

This recipe takes a bit of practice, but once you've made
one nest, the remainder will follow quickly behind. The lack
of gluten means you don't need to rest this dough as you
would regular pasta dough, although it can rest in the fridge
wrapped in cling film if that suits your timings. This pasta
dough recipe is best for use as tagliatelle only.

 SERVES 4

 TAKES 30 minutes

250g (9oz/1½ cups) potato flour
1 tbsp cornflour (cornstarch)
1 tbsp xanthan gum
2 eggs, plus 2 egg yolks
1 tbsp water
1 tbsp olive oil
rice flour, for dusting

Place the potato flour, cornflour (cornstarch) and
xanthan gum in a food processor. Crack in the
eggs and add the egg yolks, water and oil. Pulse
to crumbs, then remove the mixture and pat into
a dough with your hands.

Dust the work surface with rice flour and knead
the dough for a few minutes.

Divide into 8 rounds, flatten into discs, then cover
with a lightly damp tea towel.

Take one disc and roll with a rolling pin to a flat
enough oval to fit through the widest setting of
your pasta machine. Roll the sheet through the
machine until you get to the second thinnest
setting. Roll through the tagliatelle cutter, sprinkle
with more rice flour, then shape into a nest and
place on a tray. Repeat the process until you have 8
pasta nests.

Place a large saucepan of water on to boil. Cook
the pasta for 1½–2 minutes. Drain and toss into
your favourite sauce.

MEATY

★

PASTA

CARAMELIZED ONION
★
MEATBALLS & SPAGHETTI

A classic Italian-American recipe with a twist! Using onion marmalade gives meatballs an extra sweetness. Try to use the best-quality meat you can find, but in order to achieve a juicy texture, I'd avoid using lean minced beef or pork.

SERVES 4

TAKES 1¼ hours

250g (9oz) good-quality minced (ground) pork
250g (9oz) good-quality minced (ground) beef
4 tbsp red onion marmalade
3 small red onions, coarsely grated
40g (1½oz) Parmesan, freshly grated, plus extra to serve
10g (⅓oz) basil, leaves picked and stalks finely chopped
10g (⅓oz) flat-leaf parsley, finely chopped
a few gratings of nutmeg
3 tbsp olive oil
2 garlic cloves, crushed
1 tbsp tomato purée (paste)
1 x 680g (24oz) jar passata (strained tomatoes)
1 tsp red wine vinegar
1 x 125g (4½oz) ball mozzarella
400g (14oz) dried spaghetti
sea salt and black pepper

Place the minced (ground) pork and beef in a large bowl. Add the onion marmalade, a third of the grated onions, the Parmesan, chopped basil stalks, parsley, nutmeg and ½ tsp each of salt and pepper. Scrunch and mix everything together with your hands. Roll the mixture into 16–20 equal-sized balls and place on a plate lined with baking parchment. Cover and chill in the fridge for 30 minutes.

Meanwhile, heat 2 tbsp of the oil in a large flameproof casserole over a medium heat. Add the remaining grated onion and the garlic, and cook for 10 minutes or until softened. Add the tomato purée (paste), then pour in the passata (strained tomatoes), vinegar and ¼ passata jar of water. Turn up the heat and bring to the boil, then add half the basil leaves. Reduce the heat and simmer for 20 minutes until slightly thickened, stirring occasionally. Season to taste.

method continued overleaf...

★ ★ ★ ★ ★ ★ ★ ★ ★ ★ ★ ★ ★ ★ ★ ★ ★

★ ★

CARAMELIZED ONION MEATBALLS & SPAGHETTI

continued...

Preheat the oven to 180°C/350°F/gas 4.

Place a large frying pan over a medium heat and add the remaining 1 tbsp oil. Add the chilled meatballs in batches to the pan and cook for about 2 minutes until browned all over. Transfer the meatballs to the sauce, cover the casserole with foil and cook in the oven for 15 minutes. Remove the foil and increase the oven temperature to 200°C/400°F/gas 6. Turn the meatballs over in the sauce, tear over the mozzarella and place back in oven for a further 15 minutes.

Meanwhile, cook the spaghetti in a large pan of boiling, salted water, according to the packet instructions, then drain. Place the casserole in the centre of the table. Serve with the spaghetti, remaining basil leaves and extra Parmesan.

GRIDDLED CHICKEN

★

PENNE ARRABBIATA

Classic arrabbiata sauce is smooth, tangy and fiery! You can get ahead by marinating the chicken a few hours before you want to cook. Serve the pasta with the whole chilli in the sauce if you're feeling brave!

 SERVES 2

 TAKES 1 hour

2 sprigs of rosemary, leaves picked
4 sprigs of thyme, leaves picked
grated zest and juice of 1 lemon
4 garlic cloves, sliced
4 tbsp olive oil, plus extra for
   drizzling
2 chicken breast fillets
1 onion, chopped
1 red chilli
10g (⅓oz) basil, leaves picked and
   stalks chopped
a good pinch of crushed chilli
   flakes
½ x 680g (24oz) jar passata
   (strained tomatoes)
a splash of vodka (optional)
160g (5¾oz) dried penne
20g (⅔oz) Parmesan, freshly grated
30g (1oz) rocket (arugula)
sea salt and black pepper

Place the rosemary and thyme leaves in a pestle and mortar and bash well. Add the lemon zest, half the garlic and 3 tbsp of the oil, with 1 tsp each of salt and pepper. Bash again, then place to one side.

Place the chicken breasts between 2 pieces of baking parchment. Using a heavy frying pan or rolling pin, bash until they are the same thickness all over. Put the chicken breasts in a small dish, coat with the herby mixture all over, then place to one side while you make the sauce.

method continued overleaf...

★ ★ ★ ★ ★ ★ ★ ★ ★ ★ ★ ★ ★ ★ ★

GRIDDLED CHICKEN PENNE ARRABBIATA
continued...

Place a large frying pan on a medium heat. Add the remaining 1 tbsp oil and the onion with a pinch of salt. Cook for 5 minutes, then add the remaining garlic. Using a small, sharp knife, poke lots of holes in the chilli and add to the pan along with the basil stalks and chilli flakes. Continue cooking for a further 5–10 minutes or until the onion is softened but not coloured. Stir in the passata (strained tomatoes) and vodka, if using. Bring to the boil, then reduce the heat and allow the sauce to simmer for 10–15 minutes, stirring occasionally.

While the sauce is simmering, cook the penne in a large saucepan of boiling, salted water, according to the packet instructions.

Meanwhile, heat a griddle pan on a medium heat. Remove the chicken breasts from the marinade and cook for 3 minutes on each side until golden and griddled. Place the chicken on a plate, season with salt and pepper, squeeze over the lemon juice and drizzle over a little olive oil.

Drain the pasta, reserving a cupful of the cooking water, and tip into the pan with the sauce. Remove the whole chilli, then toss together with a little of the pasta water and divide between serving dishes. Slice the chicken and arrange over the pasta. Top with the Parmesan and rocket (arugula) to serve.

SMOKY TOMATO &

★

PULLED CHICKEN BUCATINI

Bucatini is a long, thin pasta with a hole running straight through the middle, a bit like a straw; it works perfectly when tossed through sauces. Smoky semi-dried tomatoes can be found in some supermarkets and delis.

 SERVES 4

 TAKES 1½ hours

6 skin-on, bone-in chicken thighs (800g/1lb 12oz total weight)
1 tbsp olive oil
1 tsp sweet smoked paprika
1 tsp dried oregano
1 red onion, peeled and cut into thin wedges
400g (14oz) cherry tomatoes
100g (3½oz/scant 1½ cups) smoky semi-dried tomatoes (drained weight)
1 tsp soft brown sugar
1 tsp Worcestershire sauce
1 tbsp balsamic vinegar
2 tbsp tomato purée (paste)
350ml (12fl oz/1½ cups) chicken stock
400g (14oz) dried bucatini
sea salt and black pepper

Preheat the oven to 180°C/350°F/gas 4.

Place the chicken thighs in a roasting tray. Drizzle over the oil and sprinkle over the smoked paprika, oregano and 1 tsp each of salt and pepper. Add the onion and cherry and semi-dried tomatoes to the tray, cover with foil and roast in the oven for 1 hour. Remove the foil and add the sugar, Worcestershire sauce, vinegar, tomato purée (paste) and chicken stock. Place the tray back in the oven and cook for a further 30 minutes.

Towards the end of the chicken cooking time, cook the bucatini in a large pan of boiling, salted water, according to the packet instructions.

Remove the tray from the oven and carefully shred the meat using 2 forks, discarding the bones and skin. Stir and mash everything together to make a chunky sauce.

Drain the pasta, reserving a cupful of cooking water, and tip it into the roasting tray, with a good splash of pasta water. Toss everything together and serve.

CLASSIC

★

SPAGHETTI CARBONARA

Carbonara is often added to, poked and prodded, but I urge you to keep it simple like its origins. The only thing to avoid is scrambling the eggs, so make sure the pan is not on the heat when you combine the egg mixture and spaghetti.

 SERVES 4

 TAKES 20 minutes

1 x 120g (4oz) piece of smoked pancetta (or guanciale if you can find it), cut into lardons
400g (14oz) dried spaghetti
6 large egg yolks
70g (2½oz) pecorino romano, finely grated
1 tsp freshly ground black pepper
30g (1oz) Parmesan, freshly grated

Put a frying pan over a medium heat, add the pancetta and fry for 5–10 minutes until crisp and golden. Remove the pancetta to a small bowl and place to one side.

Cook the spaghetti in a large pan of boiling, salted water, according to the packet instructions.

While the spaghetti is cooking, place the egg yolks in a large mixing bowl. Add the grated pecorino and black pepper. Using a fork, whisk to combine. Add the pancetta and whisk again.

When the spaghetti is done you have to move quickly, so get your serving bowls ready. Scoop out a cupful of hot pasta cooking water and set to one side, then drain the spaghetti in a colander. Off the heat, tip the spaghetti into the bowl of egg yolk and, using tongs, quickly toss well together along with good a splash of cooking water until pale and silky-smooth. Divide the spaghetti between the bowls and serve immediately, with the Parmesan sprinkled over.

CRISPY SAUSAGE
★
ORECCHIETTE

Good-quality sausages are already well seasoned, so you only need a few extra ingredients to make up a hearty supper. You can swap out the cavolo nero for Savoy cabbage or spinach, and the lentils for haricot or cannellini beans.

 SERVES 2

 TAKES 30 minutes

3 good-quality sausages
¼ tsp crushed chilli flakes, plus extra to serve
1 tsp fennel seeds
grated zest of ½ lemon, plus extra to serve
1 tbsp olive oil
200g (7oz) dried orecchiette
2 garlic cloves, crushed
100g (3½oz) cavolo nero, leaves torn from the stalks and finely sliced
100g (3½oz) pre-cooked brown or green lentils
40g (1½oz/⅓ cup) sun-dried tomatoes in oil (drained weight), chopped
150ml (5fl oz/⅓ cup) hot chicken stock
sea salt and black pepper

Squeeze the sausages out of their skins into a bowl and sprinkle over the chilli flakes, fennel seeds and lemon zest. Mix everything together and place to one side.

Place a large frying pan over a medium heat. Put the oil in the frying pan and add the sausage mixture. Fry, breaking it down with a wooden spoon into little pieces, for 5–10 minutes until crispy. Place on a plate and leave to one side.

Cook the orecchiette in a large pan of boiling, salted water, according to the packet instructions.

While the orecchiette is cooking, place the frying pan back on the hob (stovetop) and add the garlic. Add the cavolo nero and stir-fry for 1–2 minutes. Scatter over the lentils and sun-dried tomatoes and toss together. Pour in the hot stock.

Drain the orecchiette, reserving a cupful of cooking water, and add to the pan with the sausage mixture. Toss together, with a little of the reserved pasta water if needed, and season to taste. Spoon into serving bowls, grate over a little more lemon zest and sprinkle with extra chilli flakes.

3/10/21 — very nice, maybe more bacon needed.
+ warm plates.

COURGETTE, PEA & BACON
★
PASTA SHELLS

For a lighter version, you can use a little less bacon and swap out mascarpone for cottage cheese or ricotta. To make this dish totally veggie friendly, you can omit the bacon and use vegetarian Parmesan.

🍴 SERVES 4

⏰ TAKES 25 minutes

2 tsp olive oil
6 slices smoked streaky bacon, thinly sliced
2 garlic cloves, crushed
2 courgettes (zucchini), sliced (about 300g/10oz total weight)
250g (9oz/generous 1 cup) mascarpone
50g (1¾oz) Parmesan, freshly grated, plus extra to serve
1 tsp wholegrain mustard
grated zest of 1 lemon, plus a squeeze of juice (optional)
100g (3½oz) frozen whole leaf spinach
350g (12oz) dried pasta shells
150g (5½oz/1¼ cups) frozen peas
sea salt and black pepper

Place a large frying pan over a medium heat. Add half the oil and the bacon and sauté for 2–3 minutes until golden. Transfer to a plate. Add the remaining 1 tsp of oil, the garlic and courgette (zucchini) to the pan. Fry for 3–5 minutes or until golden, then turn the heat to low and keep warm while you make the sauce.

Put the mascarpone, Parmesan, mustard and lemon zest in a small saucepan and place over a low heat. Stir until smooth, then add the spinach. Allow it to defrost, stirring occasionally, until the spinach has wilted and the sauce is creamy.

Meanwhile, cook the pasta shells in a large pan of boiling, salted water, according to the packet instructions.

When the pasta is nearly cooked, increase the heat under the courgette pan and add the peas. Drain the pasta shells, reserving a cupful of the cooking water, and tip into the frying pan. Remove from the heat, spoon over the sauce with a good splash of pasta water and mix well. Sprinkle over the bacon. Season to taste and serve with a little lemon juice and grated Parmesan.

CHORIZO

★

ORZO RISOTTO

Orzo looks like grains of rice and is one of the smallest pasta shapes readily available. It's very versatile, due to its size, and can be used peppered through salads and, as in this case, as a replacement for rice in a risotto.

 SERVES 4

 TAKES 35 minutes

150g (5½oz) cooking chorizo, skinned and chopped
1 onion, finely chopped
10g (⅓oz) flat-leaf parsley, leaves picked and stalks chopped
250g (9oz) dried orzo
200ml (7fl oz/scant 1 cup) white wine (optional)
150g (5½oz) chopped frozen spinach
500ml (18fl oz/2 cups) hot chicken stock
150g (5½oz) green beans, trimmed and finely sliced
150g (5½oz/1¼ cups) frozen peas
sea salt and black pepper

To serve
extra-virgin olive oil
1 lemon, cut into wedges

Place a large frying over a medium heat. Add the chorizo and fry for 5 minutes until golden, smelling delicious and it has released its oils. Using a slotted spoon, remove the chorizo from the pan and place on a plate.

Keep the chorizo oil in the pan and return to a low heat. Add the onion and chopped parsley stalks with a pinch of salt. Stirring regularly, cook for 5–10 minutes until softened but not golden. Add the orzo and stir well.

Turn up the heat, pour in the wine, if using, and allow it to bubble away and reduce by half. Reduce the heat to low, add the spinach and stir in the chicken stock a little at a time. Keep it bubbling away for 10 minutes, stirring until the pasta is nearly cooked and the liquid nearly absorbed. Stir in the beans, peas and cooked chorizo and cook for a further 2 minutes.

Taste and season with black pepper, then remove from the heat and allow to sit for 2 minutes. Scatter over the parsley leaves, drizzle with extra-virgin olive oil and serve with the lemon wedges.

PAPPARDELLE WITH
★
SLOW-COOKED RAGÙ

This is my all-time favourite pasta sauce. A delicious slowed-cooked ragù made with beef brisket and pork ribs for a deep, rich flavour. This is a great batch-cooking recipe, so keep a few portions in the freezer.

 SERVES 8–10

 TAKES 4½ hours

750g (1lb 10oz) piece of beef brisket
500g (1lb 2oz) pork ribs on the bone
1 tbsp olive oil
3 celery sticks, finely chopped
2 onions, finely chopped
2 carrots, peeled and finely chopped
6 garlic cloves, peeled
3 fresh bay leaves
2 sprigs of rosemary
400ml (14fl oz/1¾ cups) red wine
500ml (18fl oz/2 cups) good-quality beef or veal stock
4 tbsp tomato purée (paste)
1 x 400g (14oz) can chickpeas, drained and rinsed
sea salt and black pepper

Preheat the oven to 160°C/325°F/gas 3.

Cut the brisket into large chunks and keep the pork ribs in pieces as large as possible. Season the meat all over. Heat the oil in a large, deep flameproof casserole over a medium heat. In batches, sear the meat on all sides until golden, then place on a plate.

Add the celery, onions and carrots to the casserole and sauté for 5 minutes, then add the garlic and herbs. Cook for a further 5 minutes or until all the water has been cooked out of the vegetables. Add the meat back to the casserole.

Turn the heat up, add the wine and allow it to bubble away for a minute, then add the stock and tomato purée (paste). If the meat isn't entirely submerged in liquid, add a little water to cover. Stir, place a piece of baking parchment directly on top of the ragù, then cover with a tight-fitting lid and cook in the oven for 3 hours. Add the chickpeas and put back in the oven for a further 1 hour until the ragù is thickened and the meat is falling off the bone.

ingredients and method continued overleaf...

★ ★ ★ ★ ★ ★ ★ ★ ★ ★ ★ ★ ★ ★

★ ★

PAPPARDELLE WITH SLOW-COOKED RAGÙ

continued...

To serve
pappardelle (allow 100g/3½oz
   dried per person)
freshly grated Parmesan
chopped flat-leaf parsley

Carefully remove the bones and gently shred the meat into the sauce, then give everything a good stir. Serve with pappardelle, Parmesan and a sprinkling of chopped parsley.

KOSHARY-STYLE PASTA
★
WITH SLOW-COOKED LAMB

The traditional Egyptian version of this classic dish isn't often served with meat, but this slow-cooked lamb and date variation makes a brilliant dinner party main course.

 SERVES 6

 TAKES 3½ hours

For the lamb
500g (1lb 2oz) lamb neck fillet, cut into 2.5cm (1in) chunks
2 tsp ground cinnamon
2 tsp ground cumin
2 tsp ground coriander
1 tbsp olive oil, plus extra if needed
1 red onion, sliced
2 garlic cloves, sliced
1 tbsp tomato purée (paste)
1 x 400g (14oz) can plum tomatoes
8 medjool dates, pitted
1 dried red chilli
500ml (18fl oz/2 cups) chicken stock
1 tbsp red wine vinegar
sea salt and black pepper

For the fried onions
1 tbsp olive oil
3 red onions, sliced

Place the lamb in a mixing bowl. Mix the ground spices together with 1 tsp each of salt and pepper. Sprinkle half the spice mix over the lamb and toss to coat. Reserve the remaining spice mix for the rice.

Place a large saucepan or flameproof casserole on a medium heat. Add the oil followed by the lamb. Brown the lamb all over, then remove with a slotted spoon to a plate and place to one side.

Return the pan to the heat, adding a little oil if needed, and add the onion and garlic. Sauté for 5 minutes, then return the lamb to the pan and add the tomato purée (paste) and plum tomatoes. Break the tomatoes down with a wooden spoon, then add the dates, chilli, stock and vinegar. Season with salt and pepper and add a little water if the lamb isn't completely covered. Bring to the boil, then reduce the heat to low, cover and simmer for 3 hours or until the meat is tender, topping up with water if it starts to dry out.

ingredients and method continued overleaf...

★★★★★★★★★★★★★★★

★ ★

KOSHARY-STYLE PASTA WITH SLOW-COOKED LAMB
continued...

For the lentils and rice

200g (7oz/1 cup) dried green lentils
200g (7oz) dried macaroni
a drizzle of olive oil, plus a splash
30g (1oz/2 tbsp) butter
1 garlic clove, sliced
150g (5½oz/generous ¾ cup)
   mixture of red Camargue
   and wild rice

When there is 1 hour 20 minutes left of cooking time, place a frying pan on a medium heat. Add the oil and onions and cook for 20 minutes until golden brown and sticky. Transfer to a plate lined with kitchen paper and place to one side.

Meanwhile, place the lentils in a large saucepan and cover with cold water (don't add salt). Bring to the boil and simmer for 8 minutes. Add the macaroni and cook for a further 8 minutes until the pasta is just cooked. Drain, rinse in a little cold water and tip into a large mixing bowl with a drizzle of olive oil; season well.

Place the pan back on a medium heat and boil a kettle. Add the butter and splash of oil followed by the garlic. Sauté for 1 minute, then add the rice and the remaining spice mix from the lamb. Cook for a further 2 minutes, then pour over enough boiling water to cover the rice by 1cm (½in). Cover and simmer for 30 minutes or until the rice is cooked and the water absorbed, then add most of the fried onions. Add the pasta and lentils, toss together and season to taste. Spoon on to a big, deep serving platter or dish. Season the lamb to taste and lightly shred. Spoon the lamb over the rice and scatter over the remaining fried onions.

SPICY SAUSAGE MEATBALLS & ★ RIGATONI

28/11/20 Delicious ✓

Good-quality sausages offer the base for perfectly seasoned and flavoured meatballs. This recipe is quick and relies on using wonderful starchy pasta water to loosen the dish. Pair with iron-rich greens and you're good to go.

 SERVES 4

 TAKES 50 minutes

6 good-quality spicy, seasoned (pork or beef) sausages (about 400g/14oz total weight)
1 tbsp olive oil
400g (14oz) dried rigatoni
1 red onion, sliced
2 garlic cloves, crushed
200g (7oz) Tenderstem broccoli (broccolini), stalks sliced into thin rounds
150g (5½oz) kale, leaves torn from the stalks and chopped
2 tsp Dijon mustard
1 tbsp chilli jam (jelly)
1 red chilli, deseeded and finely chopped
sea salt and black pepper

Squeeze the meat from the sausage skins and roll into 24 balls. Heat the oil in a large frying pan on a medium heat. Add the sausage meatballs and cook for 5–10 minutes or until golden all over. Spoon the meatballs on to a plate.

Cook the rigatoni in a large pan of boiling, salted water, according to the packet instructions.

While the pasta is cooking, place the frying pan back on the heat and add the onion and garlic. Sauté for 5 minutes, then add the broccoli and sauté for a further 5 minutes. Add the kale and cook for a further 3 minutes. Add half a ladleful of the pasta cooking water, season with a little salt and pepper, stir in the mustard and chilli jam (jelly) and turn down the heat.

Drain the pasta, reserving a cupful of cooking water, and tip into the pan. Add the meatballs and a splash of the cooking water. Toss together and turn up the heat. Add a splash more of the cooking water, if needed, then spoon into a large serving bowl. Scatter over the chopped chilli and serve.

TURKEY RAGÙ FUSILI WITH
★
FENNEL & LEEKS

This recipe is inspired by Gennaro Contaldo's delicious 'ragù bianco'. I recommend you chop the meat into 'mince' by hand; using pre-minced turkey or chicken is fine, but the texture won't be quite the same.

 SERVES 4

 TAKES 1 hour 10 minutes

350g (12oz) boneless turkey breast
   (or use chicken)
250g (9oz) skinless turkey leg
   (or use chicken)
2 tbsp olive oil
1 fennel bulb, chopped (fronds
   reserved)
1 leek, trimmed and chopped
1 carrot, peeled and chopped
2 shallots, chopped
1 tsp fennel seeds
5 sprigs of thyme
250ml (9fl oz/1 cup) vermouth or
   dry white wine
300ml (10½fl oz/1¼ cups) hot
   chicken stock
350g (12oz) dried fusilli
sea salt and black pepper

To serve
a few parsley or lovage leaves
freshly grated Parmesan
grated zest of 1 lemon

Remove and discard any skin and very finely chop the turkey breast into a small mince. Trim the meat from the turkey leg and finely chop in the same way.

Place a large frying pan on a medium heat and add the oil. Add the fennel, leek, carrot and shallots and sauté for 5–10 minutes, then add the fennel seeds and thyme sprigs. Continue to cook for a further 5 minutes or until softened but not coloured.

Turn up the heat and add the chopped turkey, then sauté for 5–10 minutes until the turkey is cooked and lightly golden. Add the vermouth or wine and cook out until reduced by half. Add the stock, bring to the boil and reduce the heat. Place a lid over the pan, slightly ajar, and simmer for 30 minutes or until thickened and the meat is tender. Season to taste.

When nearly ready to serve, cook the fusilli in a large pan of boiling, salted water, according to the packet instructions. Drain, reserving a cupful of pasta water, then tip into the ragù. Toss the pasta in the ragù with a little pasta water, if needed, then divide between dishes. Scatter over the reserved fennel fronds and the parsley or lovage, then sprinkle over Parmesan, lemon zest and serve.

CHICKEN, MUSHROOM &

★

MARSALA TAGLIATELLE

This dish is a little like a stroganoff, a comforting creamy chicken sauce with meaty wild mushrooms, lightly spiced and slightly sweetened with fortified Marsala wine.

 SERVES 4

 TAKES 50 minutes

2 tbsp olive oil
1 onion, sliced
½ tsp caraway seeds
10g (⅓oz) flat-leaf parsley,
  leaves and stalks chopped
  (kept separate)
2 chicken breast fillets, sliced
  into strips
¼ tsp sweet smoked paprika,
  plus extra for sprinkling
200g (7oz) mixed wild mushrooms,
  brushed clean and torn into
  pieces
4 tbsp Marsala wine
250ml (9fl oz/1 cup) soured cream
1 tbsp cranberry sauce
300g (10oz) dried tagliatelle
juice of 1 lemon
sea salt and black pepper

Heat 1 tbsp of the oil in a large frying pan on a medium heat, add the onion and sauté for 2 minutes, then add the caraway seeds and chopped parsley stalks. Cook for 10 minutes or until softened.

Tip the onion on to a plate and return the pan to the heat. Add the remaining 1 tbsp oil, then add the chicken and paprika. Sauté for 5 minutes or until golden, then add the mushrooms and fry for a further 5–10 minutes or until everything is golden. Add the onions back to the pan and add the Marsala. Reduce the heat and allow the wine to bubble for about a minute. Stir in the soured cream and cranberry sauce, season with salt and pepper and take off the heat.

Cook the tagliatelle in a large pan of boiling, salted water, according to the packet instructions.

Just before the pasta is cooked, put the sauce back on the heat. Drain the pasta, reserving a cupful of the cooking water, and tip into the sauce. Toss together, adding pasta water to loosen. Squeeze over the lemon juice and sprinkle over the chopped parsley leaves. Divide between dishes and serve with a good pinch of black pepper and a sprinkling of smoked paprika.

FILLED

★

SPAGHETTI SQUASH

This isn't really a pasta dish as such, but it uses spaghetti squash. Once roasted and fluffed, the flesh mimics a soft noodle-like filling. Serve this dish with a fresh green salad and lemony dressing.

 SERVES 4

 TAKES 1¼ hours

2 spaghetti squash (each about 750g/1lb 10oz)
1 tbsp olive oil, plus extra for the squash
½ tsp crushed chilli flakes
2 sprigs of rosemary, leaves picked
1 onion, chopped
2 garlic cloves, crushed
90g (3¼oz) mortadella, chopped
1 tbsp tomato purée (paste)
250g (9oz) tomatoes, chopped
50g (1¾oz/scant ½ cup) green olives, pitted and torn
90g (3¼oz) smoked mozzarella (½ a ball), chopped
sea salt and black pepper

Preheat the oven to 200°C/400°F/gas 6.

Cut each squash in half and scoop out the seeds. Place in a roasting tray lined with baking parchment, drizzle with oil, season with salt and pepper and sprinkle over the chilli flakes. Roast in the oven for 45 minutes until tender.

Meanwhile, place a medium saucepan on a medium heat. Add the 1 tbsp oil, rosemary, onion and garlic. Sauté for 10 minutes until softened, then add the mortadella, followed by the tomato purée (paste) and chopped tomatoes. Bring to the boil, then reduce the heat and allow to simmer for 20 minutes until thickened. Stir in the olives and add a little water if it seems too dry. Season to taste.

Remove the squash halves from the oven. Fill with the sauce and top with the smoked mozzarella. Return the squash to the oven and bake for a further 10 minutes or until the mozzarella is melted.

FISHY

★

PASTA

POSH TUNA
★
RIGATONI

Lightly spiced tuna mixed with sweet stewed peppers and a little lemon, with a salty kick from capers, makes a perfect light supper for long evenings. Add a little ricotta if you want a creamier sauce.

 MAKES 4

 TAKES 40 minutes

2 tbsp olive oil
6 spring onions (scallions),
    trimmed and sliced
¼ tsp ground cinnamon
½ tsp chilli powder
20g (⅔ oz) flat-leaf parsley, leaves
    picked and stalks chopped
2 red (bell) peppers, cored,
    deseeded and sliced
1 orange (bell) pepper, cored,
    deseeded and sliced
grated zest of 1 lemon and juice
    of ½ (cut the unjuiced half into
    wedges to serve)
2 tbsp baby capers
360g (12oz) tuna in olive oil
    (drained weight)
2 tbsp extra-virgin olive oil
300g (10oz) dried rigatoni
sea salt and black pepper

Place a large frying pan on a medium heat and add the olive oil, spring onions (scallions), cinnamon, chilli powder and chopped parsley stalks. Sauté for 2 minutes, then add the (bell) peppers, turn down the heat and cook for 25–30 minutes until softened. Add the lemon zest and juice, capers and tuna. Stir in the extra-virgin olive oil and keep on a low heat for a few minutes. Season to taste.

Meanwhile, cook the rigatoni in a large pan of boiling, salted water, according to the packet instructions. Drain, reserving a cupful of pasta cooking water, and add to the frying pan. Toss together with a little of the pasta water and most of the parsley leaves. Divide between plates and scatter over the remaining parsley leaves. Serve with the lemon wedges.

LINGUINE

This is a date night favourite! Simple to prepare and cook,
the fragrant shellfish mixed with herbs, garlic and chilli
smell wonderful and sweet as they steam in white wine.
Tossed through linguine, it takes minutes to bring together.

SERVES 2

TAKES 15 minutes

150g (5½oz) dried linguine
2 tbsp olive oil
3 garlic cloves, sliced
1 red chilli, deseeded and chopped
10g (⅓oz) basil, leaves and stalks
   finely chopped (kept separate)
20g (⅔oz) flat leaf-parsley, leaves
   and stalks finely chopped
   (kept separate)
8 live mussels (100g/3½oz),
   debearded and cleaned
12 live clams (175g/6oz), cleaned
10 large raw prawns (shrimp),
   peeled and deveined
120ml (4fl oz/½ cup) white wine
sea salt and black pepper

Cook the linguine in a large pan of boiling, salted
water, according to the packet instructions.

Meanwhile, place a large frying pan on a medium
heat and add the oil, followed by the garlic, chilli,
and chopped basil and parsley stalks. Sauté for
2 minutes until the garlic is lightly golden.

Add the shellfish to the frying pan, then pour in
the wine. Cover with a lid or foil and steam for
5 minutes until the prawns (shrimp) are pink, and
the mussels and clams are open.

Drain the linguine, reserving a cupful of the cooking
water, then tip the pasta straight into the frying pan
and toss with the shellfish. Sprinkle over half the
basil and parsley leaves and season well.

Divide between plates, sprinkle over the remaining
herb leaves and serve.

SLOW-COOKED ONION &
ANCHOVY PASTA

This recipe was first cooked for me by my mother-in-law at a family dinner (this lady knows how to cook pasta!), and it's been a favourite in my husband's family for many years – I hope you'll love it too.

 SERVES 4

 TAKES 40 minutes

3 tbsp olive oil
2 onions, sliced
2 garlic cloves, sliced
40g (1½oz) canned anchovy fillets
   in oil (drained weight)
40g (1½ oz/¼ cup) sultanas
   (golden raisins)
100g (3½oz) Tenderstem broccoli
   (broccolini), stalks sliced
250g (9oz) dried spaghetti
40g (1½ oz/scant ⅓ cup) pine nuts,
   toasted
20g (⅔oz) pecorino romano,
   finely grated
sea salt and black pepper

Place a large frying pan on a medium heat. Add the oil and onions, garlic and anchovies, turn down the heat and allow to slow-cook for 15–20 minutes or until the anchovies have melted and the onions are completely soft and just turning golden.

Add the sultanas (golden raisins) and broccoli to the pan. Allow to cook for 10 minutes.

Meanwhile, cook the spaghetti in a large pan of boiling, salted water, according to the packet instructions. Drain, reserving a cupful of the cooking water, then add the spaghetti to the frying pan and toss together with some of the pasta water and most of the pine nuts. Season to taste and divide between bowls. Serve with the pecorino and remaining pine nuts sprinkled over the top.

SALMON & CHILLI FILLED
PASTA SHELLS

Large pasta shells (conchiglioni) are a great way to serve
filled pasta, here with a herby, chilli salmon filling and
baked in tomato sauce. Serve alfresco, with a glass of
dry white wine and a summery salad.

 SERVES 2

 TAKES 1½ hours

2 tbsp olive oil, plus 1 tsp for
  the salmon
1 onion, finely chopped
1 x 400g (14oz) jar passata
  (strained tomatoes)
2 x 120g (4oz) salmon fillets
50g (1¾oz) smoked salmon,
  chopped
1 garlic clove, chopped
½ red chilli, deseeded and
  chopped
20g (⅔oz) flat-leaf parsley,
  chopped
10g (⅓oz) dill, chopped
grated zest of 1 lemon, plus
  1 tsp juice
140g (5oz) dried large pasta shells
  (conchiglioni)
sea salt and black pepper
salad, to serve

Place a medium frying pan on a medium heat. Add
the oil and onion with a pinch of salt. Sauté for 10
minutes until softened but not coloured. Add the
passata (strained tomatoes) and bring to the boil,
then reduce the heat to low and allow to simmer
for 20 minutes. Quarter-fill the empty passata jar
with water and stir into the sauce.

Meanwhile, preheat the oven to 180°C/350°F/gas 4.

Place a small frying pan on a medium heat. Season
the salmon fillets with salt and pepper, drizzle with
the remaining 1 tsp oil and pan-fry for 3 minutes on
each side until cooked through. Flake the salmon
into a bowl, discarding the skin, add the smoked
salmon, garlic, chilli, herbs and lemon zest and juice
and season with salt and pepper. Mix together and
place to one side.

Season the tomato sauce to taste and spoon into
a baking dish, about 24 x 24cm (9½ x 9½in). Spoon
the filling into the pasta shells and nestle the filled
shells in the dish of sauce. Cover the dish with foil
and cook in the oven for 45 minutes.

Serve the dish in the centre of the table with a
summery salad.

CRUSTED SEA BASS ON
★
ORZO SAGE RISOTTO

This is a version of a delicious sage risotto with fried lake fish from Lake Como in Italy. Orzo is used in place of rice and breaded sea bass works perfectly on top.

 SERVES 2

 TAKES 50 minutes

4 tbsp plain (all-purpose) flour
1 egg, beaten
50g (1¾oz/½ cup) dried
   breadcrumbs
½ tsp onion salt
2 x 90g (3¼oz) sea bass fillets
10g (⅓oz) sage leaves
50g (1¾oz/3½ tbsp) salted butter
1 onion, finely chopped
2 garlic cloves, crushed
1 tsp dried mixed herbs
125g (4½oz) dried orzo
100ml (3½fl oz/scant ½ cup)
   white wine
450ml (16fl oz/1scant 2 cups) hot
   fish stock
3 tbsp vegetable oil
sea salt and black pepper

Put the flour, beaten egg and breadcrumbs in 3 separate, shallow dishes. Season the flour with the onion salt and plenty of sea salt and pepper.

Take a sea bass fillet and coat in the flour, then dip in the egg and finally in the breadcrumbs. Repeat with the other fillet, then place both in the fridge.

Slice half the sage leaves. Put a medium frying pan on a medium heat and add 30g (1oz/2 tbsp) of the butter and the sliced sage to the pan. Allow the butter to bubble, then add the onion, garlic and mixed herbs. Turn the heat down low and sauté for 5–10 minutes until softened. Add the orzo and stir for 1 minute, then add the wine and allow to bubble for 2 minutes. Add the stock and stir for 10–15 minutes or until the liquid is nearly absorbed and the orzo is cooked.

Place a large frying pan on a medium heat. Add the vegetable oil and fry the fish fillets for 3 minutes on each side until golden and cooked through. Add the remaining sage leaves and fry until crisp.

Season the risotto and stir in the remaining butter. Divide the risotto between dishes and place a fish fillet on each. Scatter with the crispy sage to serve.

CRAB & SAFFRON
★
LINGUINE

An elegant and simple supper for two. Crab meat works
so well paired with fragrant saffron and silky linguine.

 SERVES 2

TAKES 20 minutes

a pinch of saffron strands
50ml (1¾fl oz/3½ tbsp) boiling
    water
30g (1oz/2 tbsp) unsalted butter
2 shallots, finely chopped
2 garlic cloves, finely chopped
½ red chilli, deseeded and
    chopped
100g (3½oz) white crab meat
50g (1¾oz) brown crab meat
grated zest and juice of 1 lemon
120g (4oz) dried linguine
sea salt and black pepper

Put the saffron in a cup and pour over the boiling
water; set aside to infuse. Melt the butter in a
medium frying pan on a medium heat, then add
the shallots, garlic and chilli. Cook on a low heat
for 5–10 minutes or until softened.

Add all the crab and most of the lemon zest to the
frying pan. Allow to simmer for a minute, then take
off the heat.

Meanwhile, cook the linguine in a pan of boiling,
salted water, according to the packet instructions.
Drain, reserving a cupful of cooking water, then
add the pasta to the frying pan and toss everything
together with a little pasta water, the lemon juice
and saffron water with the strands. Season to taste.

Divide between dishes and serve, sprinkling over
the remaining lemon zest and a little black pepper.

ONE-POT

★

PRAWN PASTA

This genius method of cooking your pasta and sauce all in one go was championed by Martha Stewart and is the favourite of so many cooks… give it a go and see for yourself.

 SERVES 4

 TAKES 20 minutes

1 onion, finely sliced
2 garlic cloves, sliced
200g (7oz) cherry tomatoes, halved
10g (⅓oz) basil leaves
½ red chilli, deseeded and sliced
300g (10oz) dried linguine
600ml (20fl oz/2½ cups) boiling
　water
1 tbsp olive oil
16 raw prawns (shrimp), peeled
　and deveined (about 180g/6½oz
　total weight)
150g (5½oz) asparagus, trimmed,
　stalks sliced and tips left whole
sea salt and black pepper

Arrange the onion, garlic, tomatoes, basil, chilli and linguine in a large, shallow flameproof casserole that has a lid. Cover with the boiling water, drizzle over the oil and season with salt and pepper.

Place the lid on the casserole and bring to the boil. Reduce the heat to low and cook for 10 minutes until the linguine is nearly cooked. Stir in the prawns (shrimp) and asparagus, place the lid back on and cook for a further 5 minutes.

Divide between dishes and serve.

CRAB, SHRIMP &

★

FENNEL PASTA

Aniseed flavours work so well with shellfish... and pasta
shells too. Prawns would also work well instead of shrimp.

 SERVES 4

 TAKES 25 minutes

2 tbsp olive oil
1 fennel bulb, about 200g (7oz),
 chopped (fronds reserved)
1 onion, diced
1 small courgette (zucchini), diced
1 tsp fennel seeds, crushed
a splash of white wine (optional)
grated zest and juice of ½ lemon
200g (7oz) dried pasta shells
200g (7oz) mixture of white and
 brown crab meat
50g (1¾oz) brown (miniature)
 shrimp
sea salt and black pepper

Place a medium frying on a medium heat. Add the
oil, chopped fennel, onion, courgette (zucchini) and
fennel seeds. Sauté for 15 minutes until softened
and lightly golden. Add the wine, if using, and cook
for 1 minute on a low heat.

Meanwhile, cook the pasta in a large pan of boiling,
salted water, according to the packet instructions.

Just before the pasta is cooked, add half the lemon
zest and the juice to the frying pan and season with
salt and pepper. Add the crab meat and (miniature)
shrimp to the pan. Drain the pasta, reserving a
cupful of the cooking water, and add to the frying
pan with a little of the pasta water. Season to taste,
then divide between bowls and sprinkle over the
fennel fronds and remaining lemon zest to serve.

SIMPLE BUT ELEGANT

★

STORECUPBOARD PASTA

Quick, tasty and ready in less than 30 minutes. Most of the
ingredients could be hanging around in your cupboards,
so it's pretty easy on the pocket too.

 SERVES 2

 TAKES 25 minutes

3 tbsp olive oil
20g (⅔oz) anchovy fillets in oil
   (drained weight)
2 garlic cloves, chopped
1 x 400g (14oz) can cherry
   tomatoes
10g (⅓oz/1 tbsp) baby capers
50g (1¾oz/scant ½ cup) black
   olives, pitted and torn
a pinch of crushed chilli flakes
200g (7oz) dried spaghetti
2 tbsp fresh breadcrumbs
sea salt and black pepper

Place a medium frying pan on a medium heat. Add
2 tbsp of the oil, the anchovy fillets and garlic.
Sauté for 2 minutes, then add the tomatoes, capers,
olives and chilli flakes. Rinse out the tomato can
with a little water and add to the pan. Bring to the
boil, reduce the heat and simmer for 20 minutes.

Meanwhile, cook the spaghetti in a large pan of
boiling, salted water, according to the packet
instructions.

While the pasta is cooking, place a small frying pan
on a medium heat, add the remaining 1 tbsp oil
and the breadcrumbs. Sauté until golden and crisp,
then tip out on to a plate lined with kitchen paper.
Season well and place to one side.

Drain the cooked pasta, reserving a cupful of
the cooking water, and tip into the pan of sauce.
Season to taste and toss together, adding a little
of the pasta water. Divide between plates, sprinkle
over the breadcrumbs and serve.

DILL, SALMON &
★
ASPARAGUS TAGLIATELLE

The shape of tagliatelle lends itself perfectly to creamy
sauces – this one contains aniseedy tarragon and sweet dill,
mushrooms and delicate pieces of salmon. Asparagus adds
freshness and crunch, but you can also use green beans.

SERVES 2

TAKES 40 minutes

1 tbsp olive oil, plus extra for the
   salmon
30g (1oz/2 tbsp) unsalted butter
2 banana shallots, finely chopped
10g (⅓oz) tarragon, leaves and
   stalks chopped
70g (2½oz) button mushrooms,
   finely sliced
100ml (3½fl oz/scant ½ cup)
   white wine
150ml (5fl oz/⅔ cup) hot fish stock
2 x 120g (4oz) salmon fillets,
   skinned and diced
100g (3½oz) fine asparagus, stalks
   sliced and tips left whole
200ml (7fl oz/scant 1 cup) single
   (light) cream
10g (⅓oz) dill, leaves picked
120g (4oz) fresh tagliatelle (see
   pages 8–13 for homemade)
sea salt and black pepper

Place a medium saucepan on a medium heat. Add
the oil and butter. Allow the butter to melt, then
add the shallots and tarragon. Sauté until softened
but not coloured. Add the mushrooms and sauté
for a further 10 minutes. Add the wine and allow
to reduce by half. Stir in the stock and simmer on a
low heat for 5 minutes, again until reduced by half.

Bring a large pan of salted water to the boil and
place a medium frying pan on a medium heat.
Coat the diced salmon fillets in a little oil and
season. Fry the salmon on all sides for 2–3 minutes
until golden. Turn down the heat, add the asparagus
and cook for 2 minutes while you finish the sauce.

Stir the cream and most of the dill leaves into
the sauce. Add the salmon to the sauce along
with most of the asparagus.

Cook the tagliatelle in the boiling water for 2
minutes or until al dente, then drain, reserving
a cupful of the pasta cooking water, and return
the pasta to the pan. Add the sauce and gently
toss together with a little pasta water.

Season, divide between dishes, sprinkle over the
remaining dill and top with the remaining asparagus.

SARDINE SPAGHETTI WITH A
★
GARLIC CRUMB

Such a bright, sunny dish, full of summery flavours.
Crisp-coated sardines served on spinach- and lemon-tossed
spaghetti! Ask your fishmonger to prepare and butterfly
the sardines for you.

 SERVES 4

 TAKES 40 minutes

4 tbsp olive oil, plus extra for the
  sardines
2 red onions, finely chopped
5 garlic cloves, peeled: 2 left whole
  and 3 crushed
20g (⅔oz) flat-leaf parsley, leaves
  and stalks chopped (kept
  separate)
50g (1¾oz/1 cup) fresh
  breadcrumbs
grated zest of 2 lemons
8 fresh butterflied sardines
250g (9oz) dried spaghetti
100g (3½oz) baby spinach leaves
sea salt and black pepper

Preheat the oven to 200°C/400°F/gas 6.

Place a medium frying pan on a medium heat.
Add 2 tbsp of the oil, the onions, the 2 whole
garlic cloves and the chopped parsley stalks,
with a good pinch each of salt and pepper. Cook
on a low heat for 15 minutes, stirring occasionally.

Meanwhile, add the breadcrumbs, lemon zest, most
of the chopped parsley leaves and the crushed garlic
to a bowl. Season well and add the remaining oil.

Place a large ovenproof frying pan on a medium
heat and drizzle a little olive oil over the butterflied
sardines. Cook skin-side down for 2 minutes, then
take off the heat. Spoon the breadcrumb mixture
over the fillets and place in the oven for 5 minutes.

Meanwhile, cook the pasta in a large pan of boiling,
salted water, according to the packet instructions.

Stir the spinach into the frying pan of vegetables.
Drain the pasta, reserving a cupful of the cooking
water, and tip into the vegetable pan. Toss with
a little of the pasta water, then divide between
dishes. Place 2 sardines on top of each dish,
sprinkle over the remaining parsley and serve.

ANGEL HAIR WRAPPED
★
PRAWNS

Angel hair pasta is one of the thinnest strands and works so well wrapped around prawns and deep-fried. A brilliant party snack served with a sweet and herby mayo dip.

 SERVES 4 as a snack

 TAKES 35 minutes

25g (¾oz) coriander (cilantro) leaves
2 limes
1 tbsp sweet soy sauce (or use dark soy with 1 tsp honey)
100g (3½ oz/scant ½ cup) good-quality mayonnaise
1 tbsp wasabi paste
50g (1¾oz) dried angel hair pasta
20 raw tiger prawns (tiger shrimp), peeled and deveined, tails left on
vegetable oil, for deep-frying
1 tbsp toasted sesame seeds

Place most of the coriander (cilantro) in a food processor, squeeze in the juice of 1 of the limes, then add the soy sauce, mayonnaise and wasabi. Blitz until combined, then spoon into a serving bowl, cover and place in the fridge.

Cook the angel hair pasta in a pan of boiling, salted water, according to the packet instructions, then drain and plunge into a bowl of iced water. Drain again and dry with kitchen paper. Take a few strands of pasta and wrap them around each prawn (shrimp). Place on a tray and repeat with the remaining prawns.

Pour oil into a deep-fat fryer, or enough to one-third fill a deep, heavy-based saucepan, and heat to 180°C/356°F. Fry the prawns in batches for 1–2 minutes or until golden and cooked through, transferring them using a slotted spoon to a plate lined with kitchen paper.

Arrange all the cooked prawns on a serving plate. Scatter over the remaining coriander leaves and the sesame seeds. Cut the remaining lime into wedges and serve alongside the prawns and coriander mayo.

VEGGIE

★

PASTA

SIMPLE

★

TOMATO SAUCE

This is the most simple pasta sauce recipe. It's a great starting point if you've never made a pasta sauce from scratch before, and it's great for freezing into portions. Use the best-quality canned tomatoes you can find.

SERVES 10–12

TAKES 1 hour 30 minutes

2 tbsp olive oil
4 onions, finely chopped (use a
    food processor to save time,
    if you like)
3 garlic cloves, sliced
10g (⅓oz) basil, leaves picked and
    stalks chopped
3 fresh bay leaves
4 x 400g (14oz) cans good-quality
    plum tomatoes, or 2 x 680g
    (24oz) jars good-quality
    passata (strained tomatoes)
sea salt and black pepper

To serve
linguine (allow 100g/3½oz
    dried per person)
freshly grated Parmesan

Place a large saucepan or flameproof casserole on a low heat. Add the oil, onions, garlic, chopped basil stalks and bay leaves, along with a good pinch of salt. Sauté for 20 minutes or until softened but not coloured, stirring occasionally.

Open the cans of tomatoes, if using, and chop the tomatoes in the cans using a pair of kitchen scissors. Tip the tomatoes or passata (strained tomatoes) into the pan, followed by ½ tomato can or ¼ passata jar of water. Turn up the heat, then reduce to a simmer. Cook the sauce for around 1 hour with a lid on, slightly ajar.

Season to taste and take off the heat. You can keep the sauce slightly chunky or blitz to your desired consistency in a blender once cooled (removing the bay leaves first).

Serve tossed through linguine, topped with the basil leaves and a good grating of Parmesan.

PUMPKIN TORTELLINI &
NUTTY BROWN BUTTER

Make the most of autumn's haul of pumpkins or butternut squash. This take a little bit of preparation, but can be done over a couple of days, and you can make a big batch to freeze for later (see *Note*, page 117).

SERVES 10 as a starter or 4–6 as a main course

TAKES 3 hours, plus chilling

1 recipe quantity Basic Pasta Dough (see page 8)
600g (1lb 5oz) pumpkin or butternut squash (about 300g/10oz cooked flesh)
olive oil, for drizzling
½ tsp crushed chilli flakes
½ tsp ground cinnamon
a little freshly grated nutmeg
150g (5½oz/⅔ cup) ricotta
50g (1¾oz) Parmesan, freshly grated, plus extra to serve
25g (1oz) amaretti biscuits, crushed
semolina, for dusting
sea salt and black pepper

Keep the pasta dough wrapped in cling film (plastic wrap) in the fridge until needed. Preheat the oven to 180°C/350°F/gas 4.

Cut the pumpkin or squash into large wedges. Scoop out and discard the seeds (or you can rinse, dry and roast these as a snack). Place the wedges in a roasting tray, season well with salt and pepper and drizzle with oil. Scatter over the chilli flakes, cinnamon and nutmeg. Place the tray in the oven and roast for 45–50 minutes, then remove and allow to cool a little. Carefully scoop the flesh out of the skins and place in a bowl to cool.

Once cool, add the ricotta, Parmesan and crushed amaretti, and mash well. Cover and place in the fridge to chill.

Roll out the pasta following the instructions on page 10.

Dust a clean work surface and tray with a little semolina and have a clean, damp tea towel ready. Have a cup of water and a pastry brush to hand.

ingredients and method continued overleaf...

★ ★ ★ ★ ★ ★ ★ ★ ★ ★ ★ ★ ★ ★ ★ ★

PUMPKIN TORTELLINI & NUTTY BROWN BUTTER

continued...

For the hazelnut brown butter
30g (1oz/¼ cup) blanched
   hazelnuts, chopped
40g (1½oz/3 tbsp) unsalted butter

Lay the sheet of pasta along the work surface and take the filling from the fridge. Place ½ teaspoons of filling at 4cm (1½in) intervals down the sheet of rolled pasta. Using a 6cm (2½in) round cutter, egg cup or small glass, cut out circles around the filling. Lightly brush water around the pasta border and fold each circle into a half-moon, pressing any air bubbles out of the parcel. Pinch the 2 corners together to form a tortellini. Place on the dusted tray and cover with the damp tea towel.

Repeat the process until you have used up all the pasta and filling. Any scraps of dough can be re-rolled or kept and made into a delicious snack (see page 118).

To make the hazelnut brown butter, place a large frying pan on a medium heat. Add the chopped hazelnuts and toast until golden and smelling delicious, then tip out on to a plate. Put the butter in a small saucepan and place on a medium heat. Allow the butter to bubble and froth, skimming off any scum, until it turns light brown. Spoon the liquid butter into the frying pan, leaving the white curd behind. Add the nuts and place on a low heat.

Cook the pasta in a large pan of boiling, salted water for 2 minutes, then drain and quickly transfer to the hazelnut butter. Spoon the butter over the pasta, divide between bowls, grate over some Parmesan and serve.

ARANCINI

Crispy, gooey, cheesy deliciousness! A great party bite you can make the day before; you'll need to let the mac and cheese cool completely. You can even use leftover Smoky Mac & Cheese (see page 154).

MAKES 24

TAKES 1 hour,
plus chilling

200g (7oz) dried macaroni
20g (⅔oz/1½ tbsp) butter
1 onion, chopped
450ml (16fl oz/scant 2 cups) milk
60g (2oz/½ cup) plain (all-purpose)
  flour
1 tsp mustard powder
150g (5½oz) extra-mature
  Cheddar, grated
25g (¾oz) Parmesan, freshly
  grated, plus extra to serve
3 eggs, beaten
160g (5¾oz/3¼ cups) fresh
  breadcrumbs
vegetable oil, for deep-frying
10g (⅓oz) basil leaves
sea salt and black pepper

Cook the macaroni in a large pan of boiling, salted water, according to the packet instructions.

Meanwhile, place a medium frying pan on a low heat. Add the butter and onion to the frying pan and sauté for 5 minutes until softened. Pour the milk into a small saucepan and place on a low heat. Stir a third of the flour (20g/2½ tbsp) and the mustard powder into the pan of onion and continue stirring for a minute until it makes a bubbling paste. Slowly pour in the warm milk and continue to stir until you get a smooth, thick sauce, about 10 minutes. Stir in the cheeses until melted, season to taste and remove from the heat.

Drain the macaroni and run under cold water until completely cold. Mix the pasta into the sauce. Transfer to a bowl or a tray lined with baking parchment, cover and chill in the fridge for 2 hours, or ideally overnight.

method continued overleaf…

★ ★ ★ ★ ★ ★ ★ ★ ★ ★ ★ ★ ★ ★ ★ ★

MAC & CHEESE ARANCINI

continued...

When ready to cook, line up 3 shallow dishes on your work surface. Place the remaining flour in one, seasoning it well, and the beaten eggs in the second dish. Spread the breadcrumbs out in the third. Chop up the chilled mac and cheese mixture in the bowl, to break down the macaroni into smaller pieces, using a couple of dinner knives.

Take a 40g (1½oz) piece of the macaroni mixture and shape into a ball. Roll in the seasoned flour, then in the egg and finally in the breadcrumbs. Place on a plate and chill in the fridge while you make the rest.

Pour oil into a deep-fat fryer, or enough to one-third fill a deep, heavy-based saucepan, and heat to 180°C/356°F. Have a tray lined with kitchen paper ready. In batches, deep-fry the arancini for 2 minutes or until golden and crisp. Remove to the lined tray using a slotted spoon. Repeat with the remaining arancini. Just before serving, quickly deep-fry the basil leaves for a few seconds and scatter over the arancini. Place on a serving plate and grate over some Parmesan.

ROASTED TOMATO & CANNELLINI
★
COURGETTI

Compared to ancient pasta recipes, courgetti is incredibly new on the scene. It's made using a spiralizer, which carves courgettes in a corkscrew fashion to produce coils of pasta-like vegetables.

SERVES 4

TAKES 35 minutes

500g (1lb 2oz) cherry tomatoes, ideally a mixture of colours
2 garlic cloves, crushed
5g (⅛oz) thyme sprigs, leaves picked
1 lemon
1 tsp coriander seeds
1 x 400g (14oz) can cannellini beans
2 tbsp olive oil
30g (1oz/¼ cup) pine nuts
4 courgettes (zucchini) or 500g (1lb 2oz) shop-bought courgetti
sea salt and black pepper

To serve
extra-virgin olive oil
40g (1½oz) watercress

Preheat the oven to 180°C/350°F/gas 4.

Place the tomatoes in a large roasting tray. Add the garlic and sprinkle over the thyme leaves. Using a swivel peeler, pare 3 strips of zest from the lemon and add to the tray, along with the coriander seeds. Drain the beans into a sieve, rinse, pat dry with kitchen paper and add to the tray. Add the oil and season with salt and pepper. Toss everything together and cook in the oven for 25 minutes, adding the pine nuts for the final 5 minutes.

Meanwhile, spiralize the courgettes (zucchini) according to your spiralizer's instructions, then place in a microwave-proof bowl and cover with a damp cloth.

When the tomatoes are juicy and cooked down, and the beans are golden and crisp, remove the tray from the oven. Microwave the courgetti on high for 2 minutes (or alternatively you can keep them raw, or stir-fry briefly in 1 tsp olive oil). Give everything in the roasting tray a quick toss, then tip in the courgetti. Toss again, divide between bowls, drizzle with extra-virgin olive oil and top with watercress.

★

LASAGNE

This is a quick and simple way of making a lasagne-style
dish without the baking. Perfect for a summer supper
– and it looks like you've made a lot of effort.

 SERVES 2

 TAKES 30 minutes

100g (3½oz/scant ½ cup)
  mascarpone
70g (2½oz) soft goats' cheese
40g (1½oz) Parmesan, freshly
  grated
20ml (4 tsp) milk
a little freshly grated nutmeg
1 tbsp olive oil, plus extra for
  drizzling
2 shallots, sliced
70g (2½oz) fine asparagus, stalks
  sliced and tips left whole
100g (3½oz/¾ cup) fresh podded or
  frozen broad (fava) beans, skins
  removed
70g (2½oz/½ cup) fresh or frozen
  peas
grated zest and juice of ½ lemon
4 fresh lasagne sheets
3 tbsp fresh basil or any green
  leaf pesto (see page 90 for
  homemade)
sea salt and black pepper

Put a small saucepan of water on a low heat
and place a heatproof bowl on top. Get a large
saucepan of salted water on to boil for the lasagne.

Spoon the mascarpone, goats' cheese, Parmesan
and milk into the bowl over the pan of water. Stir
and allow the cheeses to melt, then season with a
little salt and pepper. Remove the bowl from the
heat and grate in some nutmeg.

Place a large frying pan on a medium heat. Add
the oil and shallots and sauté for 5 minutes until
softened, then add the asparagus tips and sliced
stalks, the broad (fava) beans and peas. Sauté for
a further 2 minutes, then add the lemon zest and
juice, season and take off the heat.

Cook the lasagne in the pan of boiling, salted water,
according to the packet instructions. Drain and
place on a tray, then drizzle with olive oil.

Working quickly, get your serving plates ready. Place
a spoon of cheese sauce on each plate. Drape a
lasagne sheet over the sauce and spoon over some
vegetables, then more sauce and a little pesto. Top
with a lasagne sheet and finish with more sauce and
pesto. Repeat with the other plate and serve.

SPICY CHICKPEA &

★

SWEET POTATO PENNE

This chickpea and sweet potato sauce makes a comforting stew on its own, served with crusty bread. It makes an even better pasta sauce! Blitzing half the mixture and stirring back through helps give it a silkier texture.

 SERVES 4–6

 TAKES 1¼ hours

700g (1lb 9oz) sweet potatoes, peeled
2 tbsp olive oil
2 onions, sliced
2 garlic cloves, sliced
2 sprigs of rosemary, leaves picked
a pinch of crushed chilli flakes
1 x 400g (14oz) can chickpeas
300g (10oz) dried wholewheat penne
100g (3½oz) cavolo nero, leaves torn from the stalks and finely sliced
juice of ½ lemon
sea salt and black pepper

To serve
40g (1½oz) feta
extra-virgin olive oil
lemon wedges

Coarsely grate the sweet potatoes (a food processor with a grating attachment will help speed things along).

Place a large frying pan on a medium heat and add the oil. Add the onions, garlic and rosemary leaves and sauté for 10 minutes until softened. Add the grated sweet potato and chilli flakes and sauté for 20 minutes until it has reduced. Tip in the chickpeas (with their liquid) and bring to the boil. Reduce the heat, cover and simmer gently for 25 minutes.

Before the end of the simmering time, cook the penne in a large pan of boiling, salted water, according to the packet instructions. Add a ladle of the pasta cooking water to the sweet potato mixture. Place half the mixture in a blender, blitz until smooth, then return to the pan. Add the cavolo nero and simmer until wilted.

Drain the pasta and tip into the frying pan. Toss well, add the lemon juice and season to taste. Divide between dishes, crumble over the feta and drizzle over a little extra-virgin olive oil. Serve with lemon wedges on the side.

CREAMY MUSHROOM &
★
TRUFFLE OIL TAGLIATELLE

Experiment with different wild mushrooms (like girolles, porcini, chanterelles) to add a deeper flavour. You only need a few drops of truffle oil to elevate this dish (or add a few gratings of fresh black truffle if you can get hold of one!).

 SERVES 2

 TAKES 45 minutes

5g (⅛oz) dried porcini
300ml (10½fl oz/1¼ cups) boiling
  water
1 tbsp olive oil
1 onion, finely chopped
2 garlic cloves, crushed
10g (⅓oz) thyme sprigs, plus a few
  extra leaves to serve
350g (12oz) mushrooms, a mix
  of varieties, brushed clean
  and torn or sliced
150ml (5fl oz/⅔ cup) white wine
150g (5½oz) dried tagliatelle
20g (⅔oz/1½ tbsp) unsalted butter
180g (6½oz/¾ cup) crème fraîche
a few drops of good truffle oil
sea salt and black pepper
fresh Parmesan shavings, to serve

Place the dried porcini in a jug and pour in the boiling water. Allow to stand for 5 minutes.

Meanwhile, place a large frying pan on a medium heat and add the oil, onion and garlic. Add a pinch of salt and sauté for 5–10 minutes until softened but not coloured. Strain the porcini, reserving the liquid. Add them to the pan with the thyme and fresh mushrooms, then turn up the heat. Stir-fry for 15 minutes until the mushrooms are soft and golden. Discard the thyme sprigs. Add the wine and allow to bubble and reduce by half.

Cook the tagliatelle in a large pan of boiling, salted water according to the packet instructions. Towards the end of the pasta cooking time, add the butter to the mushroom pan, stir well and allow to bubble. Stir in the crème fraîche, turn the heat down and thicken a little. Season to taste and add a little porcini water.

Drain the pasta, reserving a cupful of the cooking water, and tip into the mushroom pan. Toss the pasta in the sauce and loosen with pasta water if required. Divide between bowls, drizzle over a few drops of truffle oil, then sprinkle over some Parmesan and extra thyme leaves and serve.

FRESH GENOVESE
★
PESTO

This pesto will keep in the fridge in a clean jar for 2 weeks, or you can freeze it in an ice-cube tray, ready to pop into dishes whenever you need. You can swap the basil for watercress or spinach and the nuts for walnuts or almonds.

MAKES 1 x 350g (12oz) jar, or enough for 8 servings

TAKES 10 minutes

2 garlic cloves, peeled
125g (4½oz) basil leaves
70g (2½oz/½ cup) pine nuts
50ml (1¾fl oz/3½ tbsp) olive oil, plus extra for the jar
75g (2¾oz) Parmesan, freshly grated
sea salt and black pepper

To serve
penne (allow 100g/3½oz dried per person)
freshly grated Parmesan
a few basil leaves
extra-virgin olive oil

Put the garlic and a pinch of salt in a small food processor and blitz. Add the basil and pine nuts and blitz again. Scrape into a bowl and mix in the oil and Parmesan. Taste and add a little more oil or cheese if needed. If not using straight away, spoon into a sterilized jar and top up with olive oil to cover. Place in the fridge and keep for up to 2 weeks.

To serve, put enough pesto into a large mixing bowl for the number of people you are serving. Add the drained penne to the bowl with a cupful of the pasta cooking water and mix together well. Spoon into serving dishes and sprinkle over a little grated Parmesan, some basil leaves and a drizzle of extra-virgin olive oil.

ONE-PAN SAUCE WITH
★
FARFALLE & ROCKET

A great way to use up past-their-best veggies: pop them in a roasting tray with some herbs and seasoning, roast, add stock, whizz up and serve with pasta. The sauce also works really well with roasted salmon and chicken.

SERVES 4–6

TAKES 1¾ hours

2 red (bell) peppers, cored, deseeded and roughly chopped
2 red onions, chopped
2 carrots, peeled and chopped
3 garlic cloves, peeled
2 celery sticks, chopped
1 x 400g (14oz) can plum tomatoes
50g (1¾oz/scant ½ cup) sun-dried tomatoes in oil (drained weight)
2 tbsp olive oil
2 tsp dried oregano
½ tsp crushed chilli flakes
650ml (23fl oz/2¾ cups) hot vegetable stock
450g (1lb) dried farfalle
40g (1½oz) rocket (arugula)
sea salt and black pepper

Preheat the oven to 180°C/350°F/gas 4.

Put all the prepared veg in a large, deep roasting tray and add the canned and sun-dried tomatoes. Drizzle over the oil, season well and sprinkle over the oregano and chilli flakes. Toss well and cook in the oven for 1 hour. Add the stock and return the tray to the oven for 30 minutes until the vegetables are tender. Blend with a stick blender, or allow to cool a little and blitz in a food processor.

Meanwhile, cook the farfalle in a large pan of boiling, salted water, according to the packet instructions. Drain, reserving a cupful of the cooking water, and return the pasta to the pan. Tip in the sauce, adding a little pasta water if required. Mix together well and spoon into dishes, then top with the rocket (arugula) and serve.

ROASTED TOMATO, BROCCOLI &
GARLIC SPINACH
★

Slow-roasted, sweet tomatoes and garlic are a perfect match. Teamed with orecchiette ('little ears') and spinach, it makes a great rustic sauce. You can pre-cook and reheat the tomatoes when needed.

 SERVES 4

 TAKES 1¼ hours

500g (1lb 2oz) cherry tomatoes, halved
4 garlic cloves, sliced
a few sprigs of oregano
2 tbsp olive oil
125g (4½oz) Tenderstem broccoli (broccolini), trimmed and sliced
2 tsp baby capers
75g (2¾oz) baby spinach leaves
300g (10oz) dried orecchiette
30g (1oz) pecorino romano, finely grated
sea salt and black pepper
extra-virgin olive oil, to serve

Preheat the oven to 140°C/275°F/gas 1.

Add the tomatoes to a roasting tray and scatter over the garlic and oregano. Drizzle with the oil and season with salt and pepper. Roast in the oven for 40 minutes, then add the broccoli and capers. Increase the oven temperature to 180°C/350°F/gas 4 and continue roasting for a further 20 minutes until the tomatoes are soft and jammy. Remove from the oven and stir in the spinach until the leaves are wilted.

Keep the tray warm in the switched-off oven while you cook the orecchiette in a large pan of boiling, salted water, according to the packet instructions. Drain, reserving a cupful of the cooking water, and add the pasta to the roasting tray. Stir together, adding a little of the pasta water if needed. Stir in half the pecorino, divide between serving bowls and sprinkle over the remaining pecorino. Season with pepper and drizzle over a little extra-virgin olive oil to serve.

VEGAN

★

CARBONARA

This isn't by any means a traditional carbonara, but it is a great vegan alternative and goes down a storm with meat eaters too.

 SERVES 2

 TAKES 30 minutes, plus soaking

75g (2¾oz/scant ⅔ cup) cashew nuts
2 tbsp olive oil
225g (8oz) smoked tofu (beancurd), cut into 2cm (¾in) pieces
250ml (9fl oz/1 cup) unsweetened nut milk (cashew or almond work best)
1 tsp light soy sauce
2 tbsp nutritional yeast, plus extra to serve
1 red onion, chopped
2 garlic cloves, crushed
10g (⅓oz) flat-leaf parsley, leaves and stalks chopped (kept separate)
125g (4½oz) mushrooms, sliced
200g (7oz) dried spaghetti
sea salt and black pepper

Put the cashews a small bowl, cover in cold water and set aside to soak for 20 minutes.

Meanwhile, heat the oil in a large frying pan over a medium-high heat. Add the tofu (beancurd) and sauté for 5 minutes until golden and crisp. Remove the pan from the heat, spoon the tofu on to a plate and place to one side.

Drain the cashew nuts and blitz in a blender with the nut milk, soy sauce and nutritional yeast until smooth, then season.

Place the frying pan back on the heat. Add the onion, garlic and chopped parsley stalks with a pinch of salt and sauté for 5–10 minutes until softened. Add the mushrooms and fry for a further 5–10 minutes, season, then turn the heat down low.

Meanwhile, cook the pasta in a large pan of boiling, salted water, according to the packet instructions. Drain, reserving a cupful of cooking water, and tip into the frying pan with the tofu and sauce. Toss together well, adding a little pasta water if needed. Sprinkle in the chopped parsley leaves and divide between plates. Sprinkle over a little more nutritional yeast and some black pepper, and serve.

FARFALLE WITH
★
BEETROOT & HORSERADISH

Simple, filling and a beautiful colour. Using wholewheat
pasta adds a nuttier flavour and keeps you fuller for
longer. You can flake in a little smoked mackerel or
salmon if you fancy.

SERVES 4

TAKES 1 hour

900g (2lb) fresh beetroot (beet),
   with leaves and stalks
2 fresh bay leaves
1 tbsp olive oil
300g (10oz) dried wholewheat
   farfalle
3 tbsp creamed horseradish
150ml (5fl oz/⅔ cup) soured cream
sea salt and black pepper

To serve
30g (1oz/¼ cup) toasted flaked
   (slivered) almonds
40g (1½oz) watercress

Preheat the oven to 200°C/400°F/gas 6.

Trim the leaves and stalks from the beetroot
(beet), wash and place to one side. Scrub the
beetroots clean and cut into cubes. Place with
the bay leaves in a large roasting tray lined with
baking parchment. Season with salt and pepper
and coat with the oil. Cover the tray with foil
and roast in the oven for 30 minutes. Remove
the foil, add the beetroot leaves and stems,
then roast, uncovered, for a further 10 minutes.

Meanwhile, cook the farfalle in a large pan of
boiling, salted water, according to the packet
instructions. Tip the cooked beetroot into a
large mixing bowl and add the horseradish and
soured cream. Season and mix together well.
Drain the pasta, tip into the bowl of beetroot
and toss together well.

Divide between dishes and top with the flaked
(slivered) almonds and watercress to serve.

WILD GARLIC SPAGHETTI WITH
★
EGG YOLK

Wild garlic is in season in early spring. The vibrant green leaves are so deliciously pungent and offer a lovely hit of flavour after winter's offerings. If making this recipe out of season, use spinach or kale, and garlic cloves for flavour.

 SERVES 2

TAKES 20 minutes

50g (1¾oz) wild garlic
   (or 2 peeled garlic cloves)
200g (7oz) spinach leaves
200g (7oz) dried spaghetti
40g (1½oz) Parmesan, freshly
   grated, plus extra to serve
2 free-range egg yolks
sea salt and black pepper

Bring a large pan of water to the boil. Add the wild garlic to the boiling water, then after 30 seconds add the spinach. After 10 seconds, using a slotted spoon, fish all the leaves out, straight into a blender. (If using garlic cloves not wild garlic, boil for 1 minute instead of 30 seconds before adding the spinach.) Season and blitz to a vibrant sauce, then pour into a large bowl.

Cook the spaghetti in a large pan of boiling, salted water, according to the packet instructions. Drain, reserving a cupful of the cooking water, return the pasta to the pan and pour in the sauce. Toss together with the Parmesan, and a little pasta water if needed. Use tongs and a ladle to create pasta nests (see page 7) and place in serving dishes. Place an egg yolk in the centre of each nest of pasta, grate over more Parmesan, season with black pepper and serve.

LEMON PASTA WITH A
GARLIC CRUMB

Fresh homemade pasta doesn't need a lot added to it to feel extra special. This fresh black pepper tagliatelle tossed in a simple lemon butter sauce and served with a crispy garlic crumb makes a perfect starter.

SERVES 4 as a starter

TAKES 50 minutes, plus chilling

½ recipe quantity Basic Pasta Dough with black pepper (see pages 8–10)
semolina, for dusting
75g (2¾oz) day-old sourdough, focaccia or ciabatta
2 garlic cloves, peeled
a few sprigs of flat-leaf parsley
2 tbsp olive oil
100g (3½oz/scant ½ cup) unsalted butter
grated zest and juice of 1 lemon
1 tbsp limoncello (optional)
150ml (5fl oz/⅔ cup) double (heavy) cream
50g (1¾oz) Parmesan, freshly grated
sea salt and black pepper

Keep the pasta dough wrapped and in the fridge until needed, then roll it out following the instructions on page 10. Make sure it isn't too thin (second to thinnest setting on the machine is fine). Roll the pasta sheet up and cut into strips by hand, sprinkling with semolina as you go, then unroll the strips on to a tray dusted with semolina. Alternatively, use the tagliatelle cutter on your pasta machine.

Blitz the bread to a coarse crumb in a food processor. Add the garlic and parsley and blitz again. Heat the oil in a frying pan on a medium heat, tip in the breadcrumbs and sauté for 5–10 minutes until golden. Spoon into a bowl lined with kitchen paper.

Bring a large pan of salted water to the boil. Meanwhile, melt the butter in a small saucepan and add a good pinch each of salt and pepper, followed by the lemon zest and juice, and the limoncello, if using. Stir in the cream and most of the Parmesan.

Boil the pasta for 2 minutes. Drain, reserving a cupful of the cooking water, and return the pasta to the pan. Tip the sauce into the pan and toss, adding a little pasta water if needed. Serve with the crumb and remaining Parmesan sprinkled over.

VEGAN

★

RAGÙ

This vegan ragù is so packed with flavour and texture that carnivores will happily devour it. Like most deep, rich sauces and stews, it's best served up the next day after marinating in the fridge.

 SERVES 6–8

 TAKES 1½ hours

2 tbsp olive oil
2 onions, finely chopped
2 carrots, peeled and finely chopped
2 celery sticks, finely chopped
3 garlic cloves, peeled
2 bay leaves
2 sprigs of rosemary
2 sprigs of thyme
300g (10oz) mushrooms, finely chopped
3 tbsp tomato purée (paste)
250ml (9fl oz/1 cup) red wine
1 x 400g (14oz) can brown lentils
70g (2½oz/¾ cup) walnut halves or Brazil nuts, chopped
40g (1½oz/⅓ cup) black olives, pitted and chopped
1 tbsp vegan Worcestershire sauce
sea salt and black pepper
penne or rigatoni (allow 100g/3½oz dried per person), to serve
freshly grated vegan Parmesan

Place a large, cast-iron flameproof casserole on a low heat. Add the oil and tip in the chopped vegetables, garlic and herbs. Sauté for 10 minutes until softened but not golden.

Add the mushrooms and sauté for a further 10 minutes, then stir in the tomato purée (paste). Turn up the heat and add the wine. Allow to bubble for 2 minutes.

Tip in the can of lentils with their liquid, and add the nuts, olives and Worcestershire sauce. Reduce the heat and simmer for 1 hour or until thickened, stirring occasionally. Season to taste and remove the herb stalks.

Serve with penne or rigatoni, sprinkled with grated vegan Parmesan. Any sauce you are not using straight away can be frozen.

GORGONZOLA & WALNUT
★
LINGUINE FINI

A fabulous simple starter packed full of flavour.
A small portion is advised, as it's so deliciously
creamy, rich and tangy.

 SERVES 2 as a starter

 TAKES 20 minutes

40g (1½oz/scant ½ cup) walnut
  halves
150g (5½oz) dried linguine fini
2 tbsp mascarpone
2 tbsp single (light) cream
100g (3½oz) gorgonzola dolce,
  chopped into small pieces
sea salt and black pepper

Place the walnuts in a small frying pan on a low
heat and toast until golden, then chop and place
to one side.

Cook the linguine in a large pan of boiling, salted
water, according to the packet instructions.

Meanwhile, pour a little water into a small saucepan
and place a small heatproof bowl on top. Add
the mascarpone and cream to the bowl and place
the pan over a low heat. Stir until incorporated,
then add the gorgonzola and stir it in until melted.
Season with salt and pepper.

Drain the linguine, reserving a cupful of the cooking
water, and add back to the saucepan. Stir in the
sauce and a little of the pasta water. Sprinkle in
half the walnuts and toss together using tongs.
Divide between plates, sprinkle with the remaining
walnuts, season with black pepper and serve.

AVOCADO & SPINACH
★
FUSILLI

Avocado pasta! Who'd have thought it!? Well, plenty of vegans have. Avocado makes salad dressings and ice creams super-creamy, so why not use it for pasta too. It's a great way of using up those ones that are just a little too soft.

 SERVES 4

 TAKES 25 minutes

350g (12oz) dried fusilli
2 garlic cloves, peeled
200g (7oz) spinach leaves
2 ripe avocados
extra-virgin olive oil, for drizzling
30g (1oz/¼ cup) roasted cashew
  nuts, chopped
30g (1oz/¼ cup) roasted almonds,
  chopped
20g (⅔oz) coriander (cilantro),
  chopped
2 limes
50g (1¾oz) feta (optional)
sea salt and black pepper

Cook the fusilli in a large pan of boiling, salted water, according to the packet instructions.

Meanwhile, place the garlic and spinach in a blender. Halve and stone the avocados, then scoop the flesh into the blender. Add a drizzle of oil and season. Blitz a little, add a splash of pasta cooking water and blitz until smooth. Leave the lid on the blender and place to one side.

Put the chopped cashew nuts, almonds and coriander (cilantro) in a bowl. Squeeze over the juice of 1 lime, season and drizzle with oil. Cut the other lime into wedges.

Drain the pasta, reserving a cupful of the cooking water, and tip back into the pan, adding a few splashes of pasta water. Pour over the sauce and toss together, seasoning to taste. Portion on to plates, spoon over the nut dressing, crumble over the feta, if using, and serve with the lime wedges.

SQUASH & BRUSSELS SPROUT
★
PENNE

This pasta is sweet and spicy. Roasted butternut squash and Brussels sprouts add an almost festive touch when mixed with cinnamon and paprika.

 SERVES 4–6

TAKES 1 hour

900g (2lb) butternut squash
1 tsp ground cinnamon
1 tsp sweet smoked paprika
2 tbsp olive oil
2 red onions, sliced
200g (7oz) Brussels sprouts
1 tsp maple syrup
1 tbsp light soy sauce
300g (10oz) dried penne
1 tsp red wine vinegar
35g (1¼oz) Parmesan, freshly grated, plus extra to serve
sea salt and black pepper

Preheat the oven to 180°C/350°F/gas 4. Peel the butternut squash, halve and scoop out the seeds. Rinse the seeds under the tap, dry on kitchen paper and spread out on a roasting tray. Season and add a pinch each of the cinnamon and smoked paprika. Drizzle with 1 tbsp of the oil and toss together.

Cut the squash into 2cm (¾in) cubes. Place in a large roasting tray with the sliced onions. Season, drizzle with the remaining oil and sprinkle over the remaining spices. Toss together and roast for 40 minutes. Roast the seeds at the same time until golden and crisp, around 20 minutes.

Finely slice the sprouts (use the sliced blade on a food processor for speed). Once the butternut squash is cooked, stir in the sprouts, maple syrup and soy sauce, then roast for a further 10 minutes.

Meanwhile, cook the penne in a large pan of boiling, salted water, according to the packet instructions. Drain, reserving a cupful of the pasta water, and tip into the roasting tray. Toss with the vinegar, Parmesan and a little pasta water if needed. Season to taste, divide between bowls and sprinkle over a little extra Parmesan and the roasted seeds.

111

WALNUT, RICOTTA & PEAR
★
TORTELLINI

Fresh, nutty and a little sweet, this combines walnuts, ricotta and pears that have just been lightly poached in white wine, and makes a fabulous starter – especially when pears are in season (or even when they're not quite ripe).

MAKES 36–40
(serves 4–6 as a starter
or 2–4 as a main course)

TAKES 2½ hours, plus
chilling

½ recipe quantity Basic Pasta
  Dough with beetroot (beet)
  (see pages 8–10)
40g (1½oz/scant ½ cup) walnut
  halves
2 pears (300g/10oz total weight)
100ml (3½fl oz/scant ½ cup)
  dessert wine or sweet
  white wine
1 clove
1 lemon
150g (5½oz/⅔ cup) ricotta
20g (⅔oz) Parmesan, freshly
  grated, plus extra to serve
semolina, for dusting
olive oil, for frying the sage
10g (⅓oz) sage leaves
50g (1¾oz/3½ tbsp) butter
sea salt and black pepper

Keep the pasta dough wrapped and in the fridge until needed.

Place the walnuts in a small frying pan on a low heat and toast until golden. Tip into a bowl and place to one side. Peel one of the pears, core and finely dice.

Place the wine and clove in a medium frying pan, add the diced pear and allow to bubble on a medium heat for 2 minutes. Grate over the zest of half the lemon. Take off the heat and allow to steep for 5 minutes. Chop the walnuts. Drain the diced pear, remove the clove and place in a bowl with most of the walnuts. Mix in the ricotta and Parmesan and season to taste. Cover the mixture and chill in the fridge.

Roll out the pasta following the instructions on page 10. Dust a clean work surface and clean tray with a little semolina. Have a cup of water and a pastry brush to hand. Take the filling from the fridge. Place teaspoons of filling at 6cm (2½in) intervals down the centre of the sheet.

method continued overleaf...

★ ★ ★ ★ ★ ★ ★ ★ ★ ★ ★ ★ ★ ★ ★ ★ ★

WALNUT, RICOTTA & PEAR TORTELLINI
continued...

Cut out 9cm (3½in) squares around each mound of filling.

Lightly brush water on the pasta border around the filling and, one at a time, fold the pasta over the filling of each tortellini to make a triangle, using your fingers to gently squeeze the air out of the pasta pocket. Fold one edge over the tip of the other and gently pinch to seal. Place on the semolina-dusted tray and repeat until you have used all of the pasta and filling. Cover with a clean, damp tea towel.

Just before you start the pasta cooking, place a small frying pan on a medium heat and add about a 1cm (½in) depth of olive oil to the pan. When hot, add the sage leaves (they will spit a bit) and fry for a few seconds until crisp. Remove them with a slotted spoon and place on kitchen paper.

Core and thinly slice the remaining pear.

Place a large pan of water on to boil with a good pinch of salt. Place a large frying pan on a medium heat. Add the butter to the frying pan, followed by the slices of pear. Sauté in the bubbling butter.

Add the pasta to the pan of boiling water, turn down the heat and cook for 2 minutes. Drain and add to the frying pan of buttery pears. Spoon the butter over the tortellini to coat. Divide the pears and pasta between serving plates, then sprinkle over some Parmesan, the remaining toasted walnuts and the fried sage leaves.

SPINACH & RICOTTA
★
RAVIOLI

Spinach and ricotta is a classic flavour combination used in filled pasta. This recipe will take a little time to put together, but you can make a big batch at the weekend to freeze for future meals (see *Note*, overleaf).

MAKES 60 ravioli
(serves 6–8 as a starter
or 4–6 as a main course)

TAKES 2 hours, plus chilling

1 recipe quantity Basic Pasta
  Dough (see page 8)
200g (7oz) spinach leaves
a little freshly grated nutmeg
grated zest of 1 lemon
60g (2oz) Parmesan, freshly grated,
  plus extra to serve
250g (9oz/generous 1 cup) ricotta
semolina, for dusting
sea salt and black pepper

For the sage butter sauce
100g (3½oz/scant ½ cup)
  unsalted butter
a small bunch of sage, leaves
  picked (about 20 leaves)

Keep the pasta dough wrapped and in the fridge until needed.

Place a large pan on a medium heat and add the spinach and a splash of water. Cover and allow the spinach to wilt down, stirring occasionally. Drain in a colander and allow to cool a little. Place the spinach in a clean tea towel (not a precious one) and squeeze out all of the excess liquid. Tip the squeezed spinach on to a board and chop well, then transfer to a large bowl. Grate over a little nutmeg, and season with a little salt and a big pinch of pepper. Add the lemon zest, Parmesan and ricotta. Mix really well and taste. Add a little more nutmeg or seasoning if needed. Cover the bowl and place in the fridge. You can do this the day before making the pasta.

Roll out the pasta following the instructions on page 10.

method continued overleaf...

★ ★ ★ ★ ★ ★ ★ ★ ★ ★ ★ ★ ★ ★ ★

★ ★

SPINACH & RICOTTA RAVIOLI
continued...

Note:

If freezing the pasta, cover the dusted trays and freeze (if you have a freezer big enough), or portion into sandwich boxes, keeping everything flat and in one layer. Dust with a little more semolina and freeze (you can then stack up for portions of pasta). Freeze for 1 month. Cook from frozen for 2–3 minutes.

Dust a clean work surface and a tray with a little semolina. Have a cup of water and a pastry brush to hand, or a spritzer filled with water. Lay the sheet of pasta along the work surface and take the filling from the fridge. Cut the sheet in half widthways. Take teaspoons of filling and dot them at 5cm (2in) intervals down the middle of one sheet. Brush a little water around each filling mound and place the second sheet over the top. One at a time, cup your hands (little-finger-side down) around each piece of covered filling and smooth out any air pockets. Use a 7cm (2¾in) square ravioli cutter, knife or roller to cut out ravioli. Place on the semolina-dusted tray and repeat the process until you have used all the pasta and filling. Cover with a clean, damp tea towel. Any scraps of dough can be re-rolled or kept and made into a delicious snack (see overleaf).

To cook the ravioli and sauce, bring a large pan of salted water to the boil, and place a large frying pan on a medium heat for the sage butter sauce. Add the butter to the frying pan and let it melt and then start to bubble; keep it warm over a low heat. Add the ravioli to the boiling water, turn the heat down to prevent them from bursting and cook for 2 minutes. Just before the pasta is ready, turn up the heat under the butter pan to medium, add the sage leaves and allow to bubble for a few seconds. Drain the ravioli and tip into the pan of butter. Quickly spoon the butter over the pasta, season with a little black pepper and serve, with a grating of Parmesan.

PASTA CRISPS WITH
★
SWEET PEPPER DIP

A great way of using up excess pasta dough; you can also serve these sweet, with icing (confectioners') sugar and fruit. Leave your pasta trimmings to air-dry for a few hours, then store in an airtight container where they will keep for a few months.

 SERVES 2–4

 TAKES 25 minutes

180g (6½oz) roasted red (bell) peppers from a jar (drained weight)
a pinch of crushed chilli flakes
1 tsp capers
1 garlic clove, crushed
30g (1oz) Parmesan, freshly grated
20g (⅔oz) basil leaves, chopped
1 tsp olive oil
vegetable oil, for deep-frying
100g (3½oz) leftover fresh pasta dough trimmings
sea salt and black pepper

Place the roasted (bell) peppers, chilli flakes, capers and garlic in a blender and blitz together. Season to taste and spoon into a bowl. Add most of the Parmesan, then stir in half the chopped basil and the olive oil.

Pour vegetable oil into a deep-fat fryer, or enough to one-third fill a deep, heavy-based saucepan, and heat to 180°C/356°F. Have a tray lined with kitchen paper ready.

Roll the dough into thin strips. In batches, add pieces of dough to the hot oil and fry for 3 minutes until golden and crisp. Transfer to the lined tray using a slotted spoon, and repeat to use up all the pasta dough.

Place the fried pasta pieces on a platter, then sprinkle with the remaining Parmesan and chopped basil, and some salt and pepper. Serve with the sweet pepper sauce for dipping.

SOUPS &

★

SALADS

MEDITERRANEAN
★
ACINI DE PEPE

These tiny pasta balls literally translate as 'peppercorns'.
Often used like giant couscous, they work so well in
salads and soups.

 SERVES 6–8

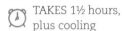 TAKES 1½ hours,
plus cooling

300g (10oz) dried acini de pepe
extra-virgin olive oil, to drizzle
2 medium red onions, peeled
2 medium aubergines (eggplants)
1 red (bell) pepper, deseeded
1 yellow (bell) pepper, deseeded
1 tsp coriander seeds
2 tbsp olive oil
50g (1¾oz) rocket (arugula)
70g (2½oz) baby spinach leaves
50g (1¾oz) feta
3 tbsp toasted pumpkin seeds
40g (1½oz) pomegranate seeds
sea salt and black pepper

For the dressing
20g (⅔oz) mint, chopped
20g (⅔oz) dill, chopped
4 tbsp red wine vinegar
1 tbsp runny honey
1 tbsp pomegranate molasses
8 tbsp extra-virgin olive oil

Preheat the oven to 180°C/350°F/gas 4.

Cook the acini de pepe in a large pan of boiling,
salted water, according to the packet instructions.
Drain and run under cold water to cool. Tip into a
mixing bowl, drizzle with a little extra-virgin olive
oil and place to one side.

Chop the onions, aubergines (eggplants) and (bell)
peppers into wedges and place in a roasting tray.
Sprinkle over the coriander seeds, season with salt
and pepper and drizzle over the olive oil. Roast for
1 hour until the vegetables have softened.

Meanwhile, for the dressing, mix all the ingredients
together in a small bowl. Season and then place to
one side.

Add the pasta to the tray of vegetables, drizzle
over the dressing and allow to cool at room
temperature for 10 minutes. Add the rocket
(arugula) and spinach and toss well. Spoon into a
serving bowl, crumble over the feta and sprinkle
over the pumpkin and pomegranate seeds to serve.

MINESTRONE
★
SOUP

This classic Italian soup is so hearty and filling, and is a great way of using up odds and ends of pasta from near-empty packets. Adding leftover Parmesan rind and sun-dried tomato paste brings extra depth of flavour.

 SERVES 6

 TAKES 1 hour

1.7 litres (60fl oz/7 cups) vegetable or chicken stock
1 leftover Parmesan rind
2 tbsp sun-dried tomato paste
2 bay leaves
2 sprigs of rosemary
20g (⅔oz) basil, chopped
20g (⅔oz) flat-leaf parsley, chopped
1 tbsp olive oil
60g (2oz) smoked pancetta
2 onions, chopped
2 garlic cloves, chopped
2 carrots, peeled and chopped
2 celery sticks, chopped
80g (3oz) any dried pasta
2 medium potatoes, peeled and chopped
1 x 400g (14oz) can cannellini beans, drained and rinsed
50g (1¾oz) Savoy cabbage, sliced
sea salt and black pepper
freshly grated Parmesan, to serve
crusty bread, to serve

Put the stock in a saucepan and add the Parmesan rind, sun-dried tomato paste, bay leaves, rosemary and half the basil and parsley. Bring to the boil, then turn down to a simmer for 30 minutes, removing the Parmesan rind after 15 minutes.

Meanwhile, place a larger saucepan on a medium heat and add the oil. If it isn't already chopped, slice the pancetta into small chunks and add to the pan. Sauté for 5 minutes, then add the onions, garlic, carrots and celery. Turn down the heat and sauté the vegetables for 10 minutes until just softened. Break your dried pasta down into smaller pieces (you can also just use the broken odds and ends from the bottom of leftover bags of pasta), then add this to the pan along with the potatoes, cannellini beans and cabbage. When the stock is ready, strain it into the soup pan. Bring to the boil and simmer for 20 minutes or until the pasta and potatoes are cooked. Season to taste.

Spoon into bowls and sprinkle over Parmesan and the remaining herbs. Serve with fresh crusty bread.

HOT-SMOKED SALMON
FARFALLE SALAD

A twist on a good potato salad, but with farfalle, and including quails' eggs, hot-smoked salmon and crunchy apple. This salad works brilliantly on its own or as part of a larger spread.

 SERVES 4

 TAKES 35 minutes

250g (9oz) dried farfalle
3 tbsp olive oil, plus extra for
   the pasta
12 quails' eggs
20g (⅔oz) bunch of dill, chopped
5 spring onions (scallions),
   trimmed and sliced
2 tbsp red wine vinegar
65g (2¼oz) Greek yogurt
2 tbsp good-quality mayonnaise
1 dessert apple, cored and diced
150g (5½oz) cucumber, peeled,
   halved, deseeded and cut into
   half-moons
50g (1¾oz) watercress
150g (5½oz) hot-smoked salmon
sea salt and black pepper

Cook the farfalle in a large pan of boiling, salted water, according to the packet instructions, then drain into a colander, run under a cold tap to cool and tip into a mixing bowl. Dress with a little olive oil and place to one side.

Meanwhile, boil the quails' eggs for 3 minutes in a small pan, then drain, run them under cold water to cool, peel and place to one side.

Put most of the dill in a clean jam (jelly) jar with the spring onions (scallions). Add the 3 tbsp olive oil, the vinegar, yogurt and mayonnaise. Season, secure the lid and shake.

Add the apple, cucumber and most of the watercress to the pasta and stir in the dressing. Transfer to a platter and flake over the salmon. Halve the quails' eggs and arrange over the top, then scatter over the remaining dill and watercress. Season with a little more black pepper and serve.

GRIDDLED SWEETCORN &
★
POSH TUNA

Tuna and sweetcorn have been a favourite partner to
pasta for many years. This recipe gives it a little grown-up
makeover. Less mayo and bagfuls of fresh, punchy flavours.
Griddling the sweetcorn beforehand adds a nutty flavour.

 SERVES 6 as a side or
4 as a main course

 TAKES 40 minutes

2 corn cobs
10g (⅓oz) coriander (cilantro),
    chopped
1 red chilli, deseeded and finely
    chopped
4 spring onions (scallions),
    trimmed and sliced
olive oil, for drizzling and brushing
200g (7oz) dried cavatappi
2 x 125g (4½oz) tuna steaks
75g (2¾oz) red Leicester cheese,
    grated
2 tbsp good-quality mayonnaise
3 tbsp crème fraîche
5g (⅛oz) chives, chopped
sea salt and black pepper
1 lime, cut into wedges, to serve

Cook the corn cobs in a large pan of boiling water
for 4 minutes, and place a griddle pan on a high
heat. Remove the corn from the pan using tongs
and place on the hot griddle for 5 minutes, turning
until charred all over. When cool enough to handle,
use a large knife to trim the kernels from the cobs;
place in a mixing bowl. Stir in most of the coriander
(cilantro), chilli and spring onions (scallions), reserving
the rest. Drizzle with a little olive oil and season.

Cook the cavatappi in a pan of boiling, salted water,
according to the packet instructions, then drain and
add to the bowl of corn.

Brush the tuna with olive oil and season well. Cook
the tuna on the griddle for 1–2 minutes each side,
then transfer to a plate.

Mix the cheese, mayonnaise, crème fraîche and
chives into the other ingredients in the bowl and
transfer the salad to a platter. Mix a little.

Slice the tuna and place on top of the salad.
Scatter the remaining coriander, chilli and spring
onions over the salad and serve with lime wedges.

ASPARAGUS, BROAD BEANS &
BURRATA

This is an ideal dish to enjoy around early summer when fresh greens are in season. Served simply with creamy burrata, it makes a great side with antipasti or grilled meats.

SERVES 4 as a side

TAKES 30 minutes

4 tbsp extra-virgin olive oil, plus extra to serve
grated zest and juice of ½ lemon
10g (⅓oz) basil
½ garlic clove, peeled
150g (5½oz) dried cavatappi
100g (3½oz/¾ cup) fresh podded or frozen broad (fava) beans, skins removed
100g (3½oz/⅔ cup) freshly podded peas
125g (4½oz) fine asparagus
1 x 100g (3½oz) burrata (drained weight)
sea salt and black pepper
crusty bread, to serve

Pour the extra-virgin olive oil into a clean jam (jelly) jar and add the lemon zest and juice. Pick and chop most of the basil leaves, keeping a few for garnish. Add the chopped basil leaves to the jar and grate in the garlic with a good pinch each of salt and pepper. Shake well and place to one side.

Cook the cavatappi in a large pan of boiling, salted water, according to the packet instructions, adding the broad (fava) beans, peas and asparagus 1 minute before the end of cooking time. Drain the pasta and vegetables and tip into a large mixing bowl.

Shake the dressing jar again and pour the dressing over the pasta and vegetables. Toss to coat and spoon on to a large serving platter. Place the burrata in the middle and drizzle over a little more extra-virgin olive oil. Scatter over the remaining basil and sprinkle with salt and pepper. Serve with fresh crusty bread.

SMOKED HADDOCK &
★
PRAWN ORZO SOUP

A little like a chowder, this soup uses potato (and cannellini beans) to thicken it. Mixed with orzo, smoked haddock and juicy prawns, it's the perfect soup for any time of year.

 SERVES 4–6

 TAKES 1 hour

250g (9oz) smoked haddock fillets
100g (3½oz) dried orzo
30g (1oz/2 tbsp) butter
2 medium onions, finely chopped
2 garlic cloves, crushed
2 slices smoked streaky bacon, finely chopped
1 celery stick, chopped
1 bay leaf
4 sprigs of thyme
1 x 400g (14oz) can cannellini beans, drained
1 potato, peeled and chopped
800ml (28fl oz/3½ cups) chicken stock
50g (1¾oz) kale, chopped
50g (1¾oz) spinach leaves
200g (7oz) raw tiger prawns (tiger shrimp), peeled and deveined
squeeze of lemon juice
sea salt and black pepper

Boil a kettleful of water. Place the haddock in a large frying pan and pour the boiling water over to cover. Allow to stand for 5 minutes, then remove the haddock from the pan and place in a bowl to one side, discarding the water.

Cook the orzo in a pan of boiling, salted water, according to the packet instructions, then drain and place to one side.

Melt the butter in a large saucepan on a medium heat. Add the onions, garlic, bacon, celery, bay leaf and thyme. Reduce the heat and sauté for 5–10 minutes until slightly softened but not coloured. Add the cannellini beans, potato and stock. Bring to the boil, reduce the heat and simmer for 15 minutes. Remove the bay leaf and transfer most of the mixture to a blender. Blitz well and pour back into the pan of un-blitzed soup, along with the drained pasta.

Increase the heat and stir in the greens and prawns (shrimp). Simmer for 5 minutes until the greens are cooked, then flake in the haddock. Add a squeeze of lemon juice, season to taste and serve.

COURGETTE, BROCCOLI &
★
PERCORNI SALAD

When courgettes are in season, their subtle flavour means
you can use them raw in this salad; griddling them releases
a nuttier flavour that matches the toasted almonds. Serve
on its own as a light lunch or with grilled fish or chicken.

SERVES 2

TAKES 30 minutes

100g (3½oz) dried orecchiette
20g (⅔oz) basil, leaves picked
½ garlic clove, peeled
3 tbsp olive oil
1 courgette (zucchini)
100g (3½oz) Tenderstem broccoli
    (broccolini), trimmed into florets
5g (⅛oz) pecorino romano, freshly
    grated
15g (½oz/2 tbsp) toasted flaked
    (slivered) almonds
sea salt and black pepper

Cook the orecchiette in a pan of boiling, salted
water, according to the packet instructions. Drain
into a colander and run under the cold tap until
just warm.

While the pasta is cooking, put the basil leaves in
a pestle and mortar with the garlic and a pinch of
salt. Bash to a paste and add the olive oil. Tip into
a mixing bowl.

Place a griddle pan on a high heat. Use a swivel
peeler to peel long strips of courgette (zucchini),
then griddle the courgette and broccoli in batches.
Transfer to the bowl of dressing. Tip the warm,
drained pasta into the bowl of dressed vegetables.
Toss with the grated pecorino, then divide between
dishes, scatter over the almonds and serve.

PASTA E

★

FAGIOLI

Traditionally served as a basic pasta-and-beans soup, the basis of this recipe is a classic example of 'cucina povera'. A hearty staple that keeps your belly full with minimal ingredients and maximum flavour.

 SERVES 4

 TAKES 1 hour

2 tbsp olive oil
1 onion, diced
1 celery stick, chopped
1 carrot, peeled and sliced
1 garlic clove, chopped
2 sprigs of rosemary
2 bay leaves
½ tsp crushed chilli flakes
1 tbsp tomato purée (paste)
2 tbsp 'Nduja paste (optional)
1 litre (35fl oz/4¼ cups) hot
    vegetable or chicken stock
1 x 400g (14oz) can borlotti beans,
    drained
100g (3½oz) little dried pasta tubes
juice of 1 lemon
sea salt and black pepper

To serve
extra-virgin olive oil
crusty bread

Place a large saucepan on a medium heat. Add the oil, onion, celery, carrot, garlic, rosemary and bay leaves. Sauté for 10 minutes until softened but not coloured. Stir in the chilli flakes, tomato purée (paste) and 'Nduja paste, if using. Sauté for a further 5 minutes, then pour in the stock and beans. Bring to the boil and simmer for 20 minutes, then remove the sprigs of rosemary and bay leaves. Ladle half the soup from the pan into a blender, blitz, then return to the pan.

Stir in the pasta, bring to the boil and allow to simmer for 10 minutes or until the pasta is cooked. Season to taste with lemon juice, salt and pepper. Ladle into bowls and serve drizzled with a little extra-virgin olive oil and some crusty bread.

HAM HOCK, LEEK & PEA BROTH
★
WITH TORTELLINI

This is a super-quick recipe using your favourite shop-bought small filled pastas or your own homemade ravioli or tortellini. Make a simple broth base and add the pasta.

 SERVES 4

 TAKES 30 minutes

15g (½oz/1 tbsp) butter
2 garlic cloves, sliced
a pinch of crushed chilli flakes
1 tsp black peppercorns
1 fresh bay leaf
1 leek, trimmed and finely sliced
1.5 litres (53fl oz/6½ cups) good-quality fresh chicken stock
100g (3½oz/⅔ cup) freshly podded peas
90g (3¼oz) shredded ham hock
250g (9oz) small, fresh, filled pasta
sea salt and black pepper

To serve
20g (⅔oz) Parmesan, freshly grated
grated zest of 1 lemon

Place a large saucepan on a medium heat and add the butter and garlic. Reduce the heat and sauté for 1 minute, then add the chilli flakes, peppercorns, bay leaf and leek. Increase the heat and sauté for 2 minutes, then add the stock.

Simmer for 15 minutes, then add the peas and simmer for a further 5 minutes. Bring back to the boil and add the ham hock and pasta. Reduce the heat and simmer for 2–3 minutes. Season to taste, then divide between bowls and top with the Parmesan and lemon zest.

VEGAN CAESAR

★

PASTA SALAD

Hearty, filling and perfect served with roasted pumpkin, this is reminiscent of a classic Caesar, but the creamy dressing is made from cashews and it's tossed with crispy croutons, capers and chickpeas, mixed with kale and pasta shells.

 SERVES 4

 TAKES 50 minutes

100g (3½oz/¾ cup) cashew nuts
100g (3½oz) stale bread, cubed
½ x 400g (14oz) can chickpeas,
  drained and rinsed
3 tbsp olive oil
1 tsp dried mixed herbs
2 tsp baby capers
3 garlic cloves, peeled
200g (7oz) dried pasta shells
250ml (9fl oz/1 cup) cashew milk
2 tsp nutritional yeast, plus extra
  for sprinkling
½ tsp vegan Worcestershire sauce
125g (4½oz) kale leaves, shredded
a little red wine vinegar (optional)
sea salt and black pepper

Preheat the oven to 200°C/400°F/gas 6.

Put the cashews in a small bowl, add cold water to cover and allow to soak for 20 minutes.

Meanwhile, place the bread cubes in a roasting tray. Pat the chickpeas dry and add to the roasting tray. Drizzle with the olive oil, season well and sprinkle over the dried mixed herbs and capers. Crush over 2 of the garlic cloves and toss. Roast in the oven for 20 minutes until the croutons are golden.

While the croutons and chickpeas are roasting, cook the pasta shells in a large pan of boiling, salted water, according to the packet instructions.

Drain the cashews and blitz in a blender along with the remaining garlic clove, the cashew milk, nutritional yeast and vegan Worcestershire sauce. Transfer to a large bowl.

Drain the pasta and tip into the bowl of dressing. Add the kale and toss well. Season to taste, add a little vinegar for sharpness, if you think it needs it, and transfer to a platter. Scatter over the croutons, chickpeas and capers and some extra nutritional yeast, and serve.

ARTICHOKE, TOMATO & OLIVE
★
ORZO SALAD

Simple to prep and very easy to eat, this picante and sweet salad goes beautifully with griddled lamb and steak. Orzo pasta brings the salad together and bulks it out.

 SERVES 4

 TAKES 20 minutes

1 banana shallot, finely sliced
2 tbsp red wine vinegar
200g (7oz) dried orzo
100g (3½oz) grilled artichokes
 from a jar (drained weight)
350g (12oz) heritage tomatoes,
 some sliced and some chopped
10g (⅓oz) flat-leaf parsley, leaves
 chopped
100g (3½oz/¾ cup) mixture of
 green and black olives, pitted
2 tbsp olive oil
30g (1oz/⅓ cup) walnut halves,
 toasted and chopped
sea salt and black pepper

Place the shallot in a large mixing bowl with the vinegar, season well and place to one side.

Cook the orzo in a large pan of boiling, salted water, according to the packet instructions. Drain and rinse under cold water.

Drain the shallot and return to the bowl. Add the artichokes, tomatoes, parsley and olives. Toss together with the olive oil. Add the drained orzo, scatter over the walnuts and serve.

BAKED

★

PASTA

PUMPKIN & CHESTNUT
★
CANNELLONI

Comforting and a little bit festive, this baked cannelloni would make a great veggie main course for a wintry dinner table. Serve with a radicchio salad.

 SERVES 4

 TAKES 1 hour 20 minutes

4 tbsp olive oil, plus extra for
  greasing
½ onion, finely chopped
2 garlic cloves, crushed
10g (⅓oz) sage, leaves picked
  and chopped (reserve a few
  whole to garnish)
1 x 425g (15oz) can pumpkin purée
50g (1¾oz) vacuum-packed
  chestnuts, chopped
8 black olives, pitted and chopped
¼ tsp crushed chilli flakes
30g (1oz) Parmesan, freshly grated
70g (2½ oz/⅓ cup) ricotta
12 dried cannelloni tubes
30g (1oz/generous ½ cup) fresh
  breadcrumbs
sea salt and black pepper

For the sauce
700ml (25fl oz/scant 3 cups) milk
3½ tbsp plain (all-purpose) flour
50g (1¾oz/3½ tbsp) unsalted butter
50g (1¾oz/generous ¼ cup) ricotta
50g (1¾oz) Parmesan, freshly grated

Preheat the oven to 180°C/350°F/gas 4. Lightly oil a 26 x 18cm (10½ x 7in) baking dish.

Place a medium frying pan on a medium heat. Add 2 tbsp of the oil, the onion, garlic and chopped sage. Sauté for 5–10 minutes until softened and starting to turn golden. Tip into a mixing bowl and add the pumpkin purée, chestnuts, olives, chilli flakes, Parmesan and ricotta. Mix, season with salt and pepper and place to one side.

For the sauce, put the milk, flour and butter in a medium saucepan on a medium heat. Whisk for 5–10 minutes until thickened. Stir in the ricotta and most of the Parmesan. Spoon half the sauce into the baking dish. Pipe the filling into each pasta tube (use a freezer bag with a corner snipped off as a piping bag), arrange in the dish and cover with the remaining sauce. Sprinkle over the remaining Parmesan, cover with foil and bake for 30 minutes.

Toss the breadcrumbs with 1 tbsp olive oil. Remove the foil, scatter over the breadcrumbs, then return to the oven for a final 10–15 minutes until golden. Meanwhile, heat the remaining 1 tbsp olive oil in a frying pan, add the whole sage leaves, fry for a few seconds until crisp, then drain on a piece of kitchen paper. Remove the lasagne from the oven, allow to sit for 5 minutes, then serve topped with the fried sage leaves.

ROASTED SEAFOOD
★
PASTA BAKE

Moules marinère meets spaghetti vongole meets pasta bake.
This is a really impressive dish that needs little looking
after, spending most of its time in the oven. Serve with
lots of bread for mopping up the juices.

 SERVES 4

 TAKES 40 minutes

3 tbsp olive oil
3 garlic cloves, sliced
1 red chilli, sliced
10g (⅓oz) flat-leaf parsley,
   leaves and stalks chopped
   (kept separate)
250g (9oz) cherry tomatoes, halved
400ml (14fl oz/1¾ cups) white
   wine
500ml (18fl oz/2 cups) fish stock
300g (10oz) dried radiatori
300g (10oz) live mussels,
   debearded and cleaned
300g (10oz) live clams, cleaned
12 shell-on tiger prawns (tiger
   shrimp), deveined
sea salt and black pepper

To serve
1 lemon, cut into wedges
crusty bread

Preheat the oven to 220°C/425°F/gas 7.

Place a flameproof roasting dish on a medium heat.
Add the oil, garlic, chilli and chopped parsley stalks,
and sauté for 1 minute. Add the tomatoes, wine and
stock, bring to the boil and reduce the heat.

Add the radiatori and arrange the seafood over
the top. Season well, cover with foil and bake in
the oven for 10 minutes, then stir and return to the
oven for 5 minutes until the pasta and seafood are
cooked. Scatter over the chopped parsley leaves
and serve with the lemon wedges and crusty bread.

CLASSIC

★

LASAGNE

A lasagne is such a crowd-pleaser. It takes a bit of work but you can get everything prepped the day before, ready to bake the next day. You can also use the ragù on page 33.

 SERVES 6–8

 TAKES 3¾ hours

2 tbsp olive oil, plus extra for greasing
2 onions, chopped
1 carrot, peeled and chopped
2 celery sticks, chopped
2 garlic cloves, crushed
2 slices smoked bacon, chopped
2 bay leaves
2 sprigs of rosemary
2 sprigs of sage
200g (7oz) **each** of minced (ground) beef, pork and veal
100g (3½oz) chicken livers, trimmed and finely chopped
100g (3½oz) tomato purée (paste)
400ml (14fl oz/1¾ cups) red wine
1 x 400g (14oz) can plum tomatoes
12 dried lasagne sheets
40g (1½oz) Parmesan, freshly grated
sea salt and black pepper

For the sauce
5 tbsp plain (all-purpose) flour
80g (3oz/5½ tbsp) unsalted butter
1 litre (35fl oz/4¼ cups) milk
freshly grated nutmeg

Oil a 30 x 20cm (12 x 8in) baking dish.

Place a large casserole dish on a medium heat. Add the oil, onions, carrot, celery, garlic, bacon and the fresh herbs. Sauté for 10 minutes until softened. Add the minced (ground) meats and the livers and sauté until just browned. Stir in the tomato purée (paste), wine and tomatoes. Bring to the boil, reduce the heat, cover with the lid slightly ajar and simmer for 2 hours. Season to taste.

For the sauce, put the flour, butter and milk in a large saucepan. Place on a medium heat and whisk for 5–10 minutes until thickened. Season to taste and grate in a little nutmeg.

Once the ragù is thickened, dark and smelling delicious, preheat the oven to 180°C/350°F/gas 4. Spoon a layer of ragù into the base of the dish, top with a layer of lasagne sheets, then white sauce, repeating the process until you end up with a final layer of white sauce. Scatter over the Parmesan and cover the dish lightly with an oiled piece of foil.

Bake for 1 hour, remove the foil and bake for a further 15 minutes until golden. Allow to rest for 10 minutes before serving with a green salad.

CAULIFLOWER & BROCCOLI
★
CHEESY BAKE

Rich, madly cheesy and the perfect bake on a cold day. Serve
on its own with lots of black pepper, and maybe a salad, or
as a side with roast chicken.

SERVES 6 as a side
or 4 as a main course

TAKES 1 hour

olive oil, for greasing
900ml (32fl oz/3¾cups) milk
50g (1¾oz/3½ tbsp) unsalted
   butter
3 tbsp plain (all-purpose) flour
2 tsp English mustard
100g (3½oz) mature Cheddar,
   grated
50g (1¾oz) Stilton, grated
50g (1¾oz) pecorino romano,
   finely grated
200g (7oz) dried farfalle
300g (10oz) mixture of cauliflower
   and broccoli florets, cut into
   small pieces
sea salt and black pepper

Preheat the oven to 220°C/425°F/gas 7. Oil a
30 x 20cm (12 x 8in) baking dish.

Put the milk in a saucepan, place on a low heat,
bring to a simmer, then take off the heat.

Melt the butter in a medium saucepan on a low
heat, then stir in the flour and mustard for a minute
until bubbling. A ladleful at a time, add the warm
milk to the pan, stirring for about 5–10 minutes,
until the sauce coats the back of a spoon. Stir in
most of each of the cheeses, season to taste and
take off the heat.

Cook the farfalle in a large pan of boiling, salted
water for half the cooking time stated on the
packet, adding the cauliflower and broccoli for
the final 3 minutes, then drain.

Tip the pasta and vegetables into the sauce, stir
together and spoon into the oiled baking dish.
Scatter with the remaining cheeses and a grind
of pepper, then bake for 20 minutes until golden
and bubbling.

8/10/21 — Yes - do again

SMOKY

MAC & CHEESE

Sweet leeks and tomatoes help balance a decadent,
creamy sauce peppered with smoked mozzarella,
paprika and bacon. Serve as a main or side.

SERVES 4–6

TAKES 1 hour

20g (⅔oz/1½ tbsp) butter
1 large leek, trimmed and
    finely sliced
4 slices smoked streaky bacon,
    sliced
1 garlic clove, sliced
½ tsp sweet smoked paprika
10g (⅓oz) thyme, leaves picked
650ml (23fl oz/2¾ cups) milk
4½ tbsp plain (all-purpose) flour
1 tbsp wholegrain mustard
100g (3½oz) extra mature
    Cheddar, grated
100g (3½oz) smoked mozzarella,
    chopped
25g (¾oz) Parmesan, freshly
    grated, plus extra to serve
200g (7oz) dried macaroni
2 medium tomatoes, sliced
40g (1½oz/¾ cup) fresh
    breadcrumbs
1 tbsp olive oil
sea salt and black pepper

Preheat the oven to 200°C/400°F/gas 6. Have ready
a 22 x 22cm (8½ x 8½in) baking dish.

Place a medium frying pan on a low heat. Add the
butter, leek, bacon, garlic, smoked paprika and
most of the thyme leaves. Sauté for 10 minutes or
until the leek is softened.

Pour the milk into a small saucepan and place on
a low heat. Stir the flour and mustard into the pan
of leek and continue stirring for a minute until it
makes a bubbling paste. Slowly pour in the warm
milk and continue to stir until you get a smooth,
slightly thick sauce, about 10 minutes. Stir in all the
cheeses until melted, season to taste and place to
one side.

Cook the macaroni in a large pan of boiling, salted
water for half the time stated on the packet, then
drain and stir into the sauce. Spoon into the baking
dish and arrange the sliced tomatoes in a layer on
top. Mix the breadcrumbs with the oil and the
remaining thyme leaves. Scatter over the top and
bake in the oven for 20 minutes or until golden
and bubbling.

BAKED AUBERGINE
★
CAPONATA

Caponata is a traditional Sicilian, aubergine-based stew that is served at room temperature as a salad. Not surprisingly, it tastes equally delicious hot and layered with lasagne sheets.

 SERVES 4

 TAKES 1¼ hours

5 tbsp olive oil, plus extra for greasing
1 onion, chopped
1 celery stick, chopped
2 garlic cloves, chopped
2 tsp baby capers
800ml (28fl oz/3⅓cups) passata (strained tomatoes)
a splash of red wine vinegar
2 tbsp sultanas (golden raisins)
2 medium aubergines (eggplants), sliced into rounds 1cm (½in) thick
5 fresh lasagne sheets
3 tbsp pine nuts
sea salt and black pepper

To serve
5g (⅛oz) basil leaves
20g (⅔oz) Parmesan, freshly grated

Preheat the oven to 200°C/400°F/gas 6. Oil a baking dish, about 27 x 21cm (10¾ x 8¼in).

Place a medium saucepan on a medium heat. Add 1 tbsp of the oil, the onion, celery and garlic. Sauté for 10 minutes until softened but not coloured. Stir in the capers, passata (strained tomatoes), vinegar and sultanas (golden raisins). Bring to the boil, then reduce the heat and simmer for 20 minutes.

Meanwhile, place a large frying pan on a medium heat and add the remaining 4 tbsp oil. Fry the aubergine (eggplant) slices in batches on each side until golden, place on a plate and keep to one side.

Season the sauce to taste. Spoon a third of the sauce into the base of the oiled baking dish. Cover with a layer of lasagne sheets and then a layer of aubergine slices. Scatter over a few pine nuts, reserving some for the top, and repeat the process until you have the final layer of sauce at the top of the dish. Scatter with the remaining pine nuts, then bake for 20 minutes until cooked and bubbling. Serve with basil leaves and a sprinkling of freshly grated Parmesan scattered on top.

LASAGNE WITH
★
WINTER GREENS & FONTINA

A real winter warmer using readily available winter greens.
There isn't a huge amount of pasta in this recipe, so it would
work really well as an accompaniment to a roast dinner.

 SERVES 4

 TAKES 1 hour

2 tbsp olive oil, plus extra for
    greasing
300g (10oz) Savoy cabbage, stalks
    removed, leaves torn
100g (3½oz) kale, stalks removed,
    leaves torn
900ml (32fl oz/3¾ cups) milk
3½ tbsp plain (all-purpose) flour
50g (1¾oz/3½ tbsp) unsalted
    butter
50g (1¾oz/scant ¼ cup) ricotta
30g (1oz) Parmesan, freshly grated
100g (3½oz) fontina or taleggio, cut
    into cubes
2 garlic cloves, sliced
6 fresh lasagne sheets (about
    165g/5¾oz)
sea salt and black pepper

Preheat the oven to 180°C/350°F/gas 4. Lightly oil a
large baking dish.

Bring a large pan of water to the boil, add the
cabbage and cook for 2 minutes. Remove using tongs,
place on a plate and pat the leaves dry.

Place the kale in a large roasting tray, toss with the oil
and season. Roast for 15 minutes or until crisp, then
remove and place to one side. Increase the oven
temperature to 200°C/400°F/gas 6.

Meanwhile, put the milk in a medium saucepan and
add the flour and butter. Whisk slowly on a low heat
for about 5–10 minutes until the sauce coats the
back of a spoon. Stir in the ricotta and most of the
Parmesan. Stir in the cubes of fontina or taleggio and
the garlic. Season to taste.

Distribute a layer of cabbage on the base of the oiled
baking dish. Add half the lasagne sheets in an even
layer, spoon a third of the sauce on top and sprinkle
with a little crispy kale. Cover with another layer of
cabbage leaves, lasagne sheets, sauce and kale, then
finish with a layer of sauce (reserving a little kale). Bake
for 20 minutes until golden and bubbling, then scatter
over the reserved kale and Parmesan before serving.

BUTTERNUT SQUASH & HAZELNUT BRAISED PASTA

This recipe is a hybrid of a pasta bake, stew and soup.
The sauce is much lighter and contains no dairy but is still
very comforting and can be eaten out of a bowl.

 SERVES 4–6

 TAKES 1½ hours

100g (3½oz) spicy cooking chorizo,
  sliced
a little olive oil
2 onions, chopped
2 garlic cloves, crushed
½ tsp ground cinnamon
850g (1lb 14oz) butternut squash,
  peeled, deseeded and cut into
  1cm (½in) cubes
700ml (25fl oz/3 cups) hot chicken
  stock
300g (10oz) dried rigatoni
30g (1oz/¼ cup) hazelnuts,
  chopped
extra-virgin olive oil, for drizzling
sea salt and black pepper
20g (⅔oz) rocket (arugula),
  to serve

Have ready a 26 x 20cm (10½ x 8in) baking dish.

Place a frying pan on a medium heat, add the
chorizo and fry until golden and starting to crisp.
Transfer to a bowl and place to one side. Return
the pan to the heat, add a little olive oil if needed,
then sauté the onions, garlic and cinnamon for
10 minutes until softened. Add the squash and sauté
for a further 20 minutes, stirring regularly. Add the
stock, bring to the boil, reduce the heat and simmer
for 10 minutes until the squash is cooked.

Meanwhile, cook the rigatoni for half the cooking
time stated on the packet. Drain and place to one
side. Preheat the oven to 180°C/350°F/gas 4.

Remove about a quarter of the cooked squash
cubes. Add the remaining contents of the pan to
a blender and season to taste. Blitz to a smooth
sauce, then spoon half the sauce into the baking
dish. Add the pasta, then spoon over the reserved
squash cubes and the chorizo. Top with the rest of
the sauce and the chopped hazelnuts. Cover with
an oiled sheet of foil and bake for 20 minutes, then
remove the foil and bake for a further 15 minutes
until golden. Finish with a drizzle of extra-virgin
olive oil and serve with the rocket (arugula).

AUBERGINE, PEPPER & COURGETTE
★
PASTA CAKE

A great recipe to have hot or cold – take it on a picnic and serve, cut into slices, with salad. Easy to put together and a really delicious and unusual way of serving a pasta bake.

 SERVES 4–6

 TAKES 1½ hours, plus resting

4 tbsp olive oil, plus extra for greasing
1 medium courgette (zucchini), chopped
1 small aubergine (eggplant), chopped
1 red (bell) pepper, cored, deseeded and sliced
2 tsp dried mixed herbs
1 onion, chopped
2 garlic cloves, crushed
2 slices smoked streaky bacon, chopped (optional)
50g (1¾oz/scant ½ cup) smoky semi-dried tomatoes (drained weight), chopped
1 x 400g (14oz) can plum tomatoes
200g (7oz) dried rigatoni or any dried pasta
15g (½oz) Parmesan, freshly grated, plus extra to serve
10g (⅓oz) basil, leaves picked
sea salt and black pepper

Lightly oil a 20cm (8in) springform cake tin (pan) and line the base with baking parchment.

Place a frying pan on a medium heat. Add 2 tbsp of the oil and, in batches, sauté the courgette (zucchini), aubergine (eggplant) and (bell) pepper until golden. Place in a large bowl with the dried mixed herbs and season to taste.

Place a saucepan on a medium heat. Add 1 tbsp oil, the onion, garlic and bacon, if using. Sauté for 10 minutes. Add the semi-dried and canned tomatoes, bring to the boil and reduce to a simmer. Cook for 20 minutes or until thickened. Season to taste. Preheat the oven to 180°C/350°F/gas 4.

Cook the pasta according to the packet instructions, drain and add to the bowl of vegetables, along with the sauce. Mix and let sit for 5 minutes. Add the Parmesan, spoon the pasta into the oiled tin, cover with foil and bake for 40 minutes until golden.

Remove from the oven and allow to sit for 15 minutes. Place a frying pan on a medium heat and fry the basil leaves in the remaining 1 tbsp olive oil. Turn the cake out on to a board and sprinkle over the Parmesan and fried basil leaves.

RICOTTA & SAUSAGE

★

BAKED PENNE ZITI

A take on a simple cheese and tomato pasta bake. The sauce is boosted with crispy sausage meat and the cheese element is lemony ricotta. Ziti is a variation of penne.

 SERVES 4

 TAKES 1¼ hours

2 tbsp olive oil, plus extra for greasing
3 pork sausages
1 onion, chopped
3 garlic cloves, crushed
10g (⅓oz) basil, leaves picked and stalks chopped
2 x 400g (14oz) cans plum tomatoes
300g (10oz) dried penne ziti
50g (1¾oz) baby spinach leaves
150g (5½oz/⅔ cup) ricotta
grated zest of 1 lemon
30g (1oz) Parmesan, freshly grated
sea salt and black pepper

Preheat the oven to 180°C/350°F/gas 4. Lightly oil a 26 x 18cm (10½ x 7in) baking dish.

Place a frying pan on a medium heat. Squeeze the sausages from their skins and add to the frying pan. Break up the meat with the back of a wooden spoon and sauté for 5 minutes or until golden. Spoon into a bowl and place to one side.

Place the pan back on the heat. Add the oil, onion, garlic and chopped basil stalks. Sauté for 10 minutes, then add the tomatoes and half the basil leaves. Half-fill the empty tomato can with water and add this too. Mash the tomatoes with the back of a wooden spoon, bring to the boil, reduce to a simmer and allow to bubble away for 20 minutes.

Cook the ziti for half the cooking time stated on the packet, then drain. Stir the spinach and sausage meat into the sauce and season to taste.

Mix the ricotta and lemon zest together with half the Parmesan. Spoon half the sauce into the oiled baking dish, sprinkle over the pasta and cover with the remaining sauce. Dot over the ricotta mixture and remaining Parmesan. Bake for 25 minutes until bubbling. Scatter with the basil leaves and serve.

SPICED ANGEL HAIR WITH
★
ROASTED PLUMS

The subtle spices and sweetness of baked angel hair pasta
in coconut milk, offset with roasted plums and apricots,
create a dish vaguely reminiscent of sweet treats from
the north of India.

SERVES 4–6

TAKES 1 hour

unsalted butter, for greasing
6 plums (or apricots), halved
   and stoned
150ml (5fl oz/⅔ cup) apple juice
250g (9oz) dried angel hair pasta,
   broken into quarters
2 cardamom pods, crushed
1 cinnamon stick
2 cloves
2 x 400g (14oz) cans coconut milk
200ml (7fl oz /generous ¾ cup)
   milk or water
2 pieces of stem ginger in syrup,
   chopped
a little freshly grated nutmeg
grated zest of 1 lemon
70g (2½oz/generous ½ cup)
   shelled pistachios, chopped

Preheat the oven to 180°C/350°F/gas 4. Lightly
butter a 26 x 18cm (10½ x 7in) baking dish.

Place the fruit in a small roasting dish, pour over
the apple juice and roast in the oven for 30 minutes
until softened. Every so often, remove the tray of
fruit from the oven and spoon the juice over the
fruit. Remove and set aside until ready to serve.

Meanwhile, place the angel hair in a large roasting
tray, add the spices and roast in the oven for 5
minutes until the pasta is golden. Set aside to cool.

Put the coconut milk in a medium saucepan with
the milk or water. Add the ginger, nutmeg and
lemon zest. Simmer and stir over a low heat.

Place the pasta and spices in the greased dish.
Pour the infused coconut milk over the pasta and
sprinkle over 50g (1¾oz) of the pistachios.

Mix together well and cover the dish with foil. Bake
for 20 minutes, then remove the foil and bake for a
further 10 minutes or until golden and bubbling.

Sprinkle over the remaining pistachios, portion into
bowls and serve with the roasted fruit.

ORZO PUDDING WITH
★
BALSAMIC BERRIES

Similar to a rice pudding, this baked orzo pudding
contains juicy berries and is served with peppery poached
strawberries, basil sugar and toasted flaked almonds. Eat
hot or cold, with everyone helping themselves to toppings.

 SERVES 4

 TAKES 1 hour

unsalted butter, for greasing
300ml (10½fl oz/1¼ cups) double
   (heavy) cream
400ml (14fl oz/1¾ cups) milk
1 tsp vanilla bean paste
1 tbsp Amaretto liqueur (optional)
1 egg
130g (4½oz/⅔ cup) caster
   (superfine) sugar
200g (7oz) dried orzo
600g (1lb 5oz) strawberries and
   mixed berries, hulled and
   quartered
10g (⅓oz) basil leaves
a splash of balsamic vinegar
a good pinch of black pepper
40g (1½oz/⅓ cup) toasted flaked
   (slivered) almonds

Preheat the oven to 180°C/350°F/gas 4. Butter a
23cm (9in) baking dish.

Add the cream, milk, vanilla and Amaretto, if using,
to a medium saucepan on a low heat. Stir until the
cream gently steams. Place the egg in a large mixing
bowl and whisk with 2 tbsp of the sugar until light
and fluffy. Slowly pour the cream and milk mixture
into the egg, whisking continuously. Stir in the orzo
and a third of the strawberries and berries, return
to the pan and stir on a low heat for 5 minutes.

Pour the mixture into the greased baking dish and
bake in the oven for 40 minutes or until set.

Meanwhile, place the basil leaves in a pestle and
mortar and grind with the remaining sugar. Spoon
into a dish and place to one side.

Put the remaining strawberries and berries into a
small saucepan and add the vinegar and pepper.
Place on a low heat and poach for 5–10 minutes.

When the orzo is ready, remove from the oven
and sprinkle over the almonds. Allow to rest for
2 minutes, then serve with the basil sugar and
poached berries.

INDEX

★★

ACKNOWLEDGEMENTS

Thank you so much to Libby Silbermann and Jake Fenton for being brilliant assistants as always.

Thank you Faith Mason for working your photography magic and to Rachel Vere for perfect propping. To the lovely team at Quadrille; Harry, Alicia, Claire and Sarah thank you for your support, word wrangling, design and organisation.

Thank you Benedict for all your love, support and enthusiasm as always.

ABOUT THE AUTHOR

Pip Spence is a food stylist and writer who worked with the Jamie Oliver Food Team for 8 years. She has worked around the world on bestselling food publications and international television programmes, as well as setting up cookery demos and menu styling for major companies and chefs. This is her second book.